MATTERS OF LIFE AND DEATH

EDWARD F. DOLAN, JR.

MATTERS OF LIFE AND DEATH

FRANKLIN WATTS
NEW YORK | LONDON | TORONTO | SYDNEY | 1982
AN IMPACT BOOK

Library of Congress Cataloging in Publication Data

Dolan, Edward F., 1924-
Matters of life and death.

(An Impact book)
Bibliography: p.
Includes index,
Summary: Presents the controversial topics of
abortion, euthanasia, and test tube births.
1. Abortion—Moral and ethical aspects—Juvenile
literature.   2. Euthanasia—Moral and ethical aspects—
Juvenile literature.   3. Fertilization in vitro, Human—
Moral and ethical aspects—Juvenile literature. [1. Abortion
—Moral and ethical aspects.   2. Euthanasia—Moral and ethical
aspects.   3. Test tube babies—Moral and ethical aspects]   I. Title.
HQ767.3.D6   1982   176   82-13656
ISBN 0-531-04497-1

CONTENTS

I am indebted to many people for their help in the preparation of this book. In particular, thanks must go to William Royse for his editorial comment; to Thomas Scully, M.D., for answering particular medical questions; to the office of Congressman John Burton of California for providing needed information; and to Carol Levine and Roselle Shubin for their review of the manuscript.

I must also thank the following organizations for their cooperation in providing specific points of information or indicating where the material could be obtained: the National Abortion Rights Action League and the Planned Parenthood Associations of San Francisco, Marin County, and Contra Costa County, all of California.

Finally, I wish to acknowledge with gratitude the permission to quote from the following sources: .

Excerpts from "Should Abortion Be Allowed?", a copyrighted interview in *U.S. News & World Report* of May 4, 1981.

The living-will excerpt from "Personal Directions for Care at the End of Life" by Sissela Bok, reprinted by permission of *The New England Journal of Medicine* (vol. 295, pages 367–369, August 12, 1976).

FOR MARGARET SCARIANO
Fine friend, fine teacher

PREFACE

Abortion . . . contraception
. . . euthanasia . . . in vitro fertilization . . . artificial insemination . . . cloning.

Some of these terms are familiar to everyone; some
are strange to our ears. Some are as old as the human race,
and some have come into the language just recently. But
they all have two characteristics in common.

First, they are terms of vital importance to each of us.
They all have to do with that most precious of our posses-
sions—our lives.

Second, they have all caused public controversies.
These controversies have been significant because they
are concerned with our power over human life. They ask
questions that none of us can ignore. Do we have the right
to determine that a human being should not be born? Do
we have the right to determine that a human being can be
conceived in a manner other than by sexual intercourse?
Do we have the right to determine that a fellow human
being should die?

The purpose of this book is to look at these various controversies so that, in the light of what you learn, you can make up your mind where you stand on them and then perhaps make some contribution toward their solution.

In the main, we're going to look at three of the most heated controversies and talk about the others as we go along. The first of the three concerns the practice of abortion. The issue of abortion has divided millions of people into opposing camps. It concerns the question of whether or not we have the right to prevent a conceived but as yet unborn life from being born. Is that prevention of life, as many people believe, murder? Or is it, at least sometimes, a morally acceptable and even humane act when the circumstances that cause a woman to have an abortion are taken into consideration?

The second of today's great controversies centers on euthanasia, which has often been called "mercy killing." One specific type of euthanasia is at the heart of the current debate—namely, the withholding or withdrawal of some life-sustaining measure developed by modern medicine and used in a situation where an incurable disease has doomed a patient to a prolonged and often agonizing death. People are divided over the question of whether or not we have the right to hasten death—to end a precious life—in the name of saving the patient further suffering. Is that an act of murder or of compassion?

These two controversies have been raging for years and may well be coming to some kind of legal solution in the 1980s. But the third controversy is quite new. It concerns the issue of "test tube babies" or, to be more specific, a new medical procedure called *in vitro fertilization*. This procedure has resulted in a number of successful births in Great Britain, Australia, and the United States, and is being applauded and condemned all at the same time. It forces us to question whether it is morally right to conceive human life as a result of a medical procedure in a laboratory rather than an act of love and in the natural environment of the mother's womb.

[2]

At the same time, we'll look briefly at two subjects that have caused a lesser degree of controversy. One is another "test tube baby" procedure called artificial insemination. It was first used in the eighteenth century and has not been much discussed in recent years, perhaps because it has been practiced for so long or perhaps because most people have heard little about it. It may become a major source of debate, however, since it is similar to the widely reported in vitro fertilization process.

The second topic is cloning, which is the process by which genetically identical life forms are produced in a laboratory. It has not become a matter of widespread debate because it is still in the experimental stage and has been used only with lower and very basic life forms. The cloning of human beings is presently in the realm of science-fiction. But, as science develops, cloning may involve the development of human life, at which time it will certainly become a matter of heated debate.

And so these are all controversies that we must think about and try to solve because they can affect us all. They are, indeed, matters of life and death.

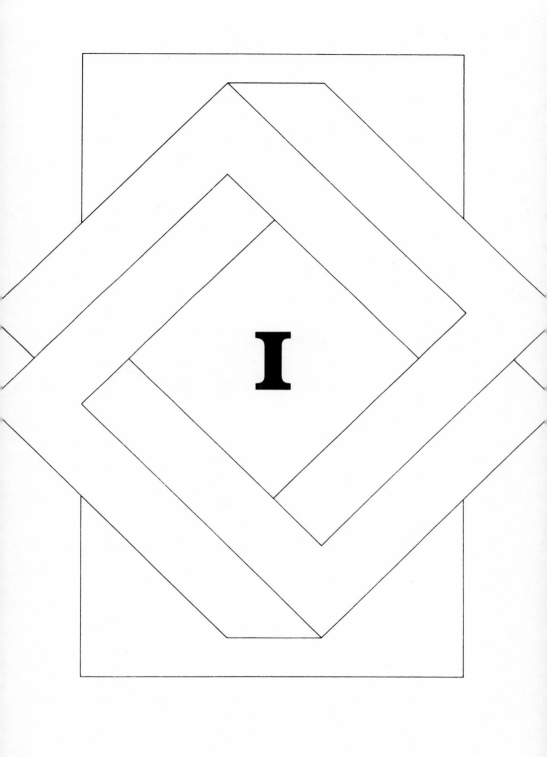

THE ABORTION CONTROVERSY

If you've ever attended a class in sex education or human biology, you know the meaning of the word behind the first great controversy to be discussed. *Abortion* is a word that can easily be defined. It means the loss of an unborn child from the mother's uterus.

An unborn child is called an *embryo* in the earliest stages of its development. At the end of eight weeks its skeleton begins to take shape, as do its arms, legs, and vital organs. The child now becomes known as a *fetus*. Abortion, then, may involve the loss of either an embryo or a fetus. In this book, though, for the sake of easier reading, we'll use just the word fetus.

There are two kinds of abortion. First, a mother may lose her fetus in what are called "spontaneous" ways. Perhaps she has an accident, such as a bad fall, that dislodges the fetus from its place within her. Perhaps she is taken ill or develops an infection that causes the fetus to be expelled from the uterus. Or pehaps nature itself may cause the fetus to be expelled because it is growing in an abnormal manner. By far the greatest number of spontaneous abortions are caused by fetuses that are malformed and thus growing in an abnormal way.

At least 15 percent of all diagnosed pregnancies result in spontaneous abortions. Such abortions occur mostly among older couples and among women who have had difficulty becoming pregnant or who have suffered a previous abortion.

When physicians speak of spontaneous abortion, they are talking about the loss of the fetus during the first three months of pregnancy, the time when about 90 percent of all abortions occur. A loss during these months is also called a *miscarriage*. It's permissible to use the term miscarriage here, but technically, miscarriage means the spontaneous loss of a fetus during the fourth through the sixth month of pregnancy. If a child is born between the sixth month and the normal birth date in the ninth month, it is said to be *premature*. If a child is born dead at any time after the sixth month, it is referred to as being *stillborn*.

The second type of abortion is termed *induced*. This means that the fetus is deliberately made—induced—to leave the uterus. It can be removed either by surgical or chemical means. Any of several operations may be performed. In one very common procedure, the doctor widens the opening of the uterus with surgical instruments called dilators and then extracts the fetus with special instruments. Another method calls for the doctor to insert a small tube with a hole near the end and take the fetus out by suction. Using yet another method, the physician may wash the uterus with a salt or sugar solution that replaces the natural fluid around the fetus; this causes labor contractions in twenty to twenty-four hours. The fetus then leaves the uterus in the same way that a child would have left had it been allowed to develop and be born.

Induced abortions are most safely performed in the beginning stages of pregnancy, when the fetus is quite

[8]

small. The best time is within the first three months, or, as it is technically called, the *first trimester*. But induced abortions are sometimes performed very late in the second three months—the *second trimester*.

Each year countless women around the world, willingly and happily, give birth to their babies. Many other women are unwilling or feel unable to bear the children that are taking shape within them, and they have induced abortions. The reasons for wanting an induced abortion can be many. The mother's health or even her life may be in danger if she continues to carry the child. She may not want the child because she is unmarried or is pregnant as a result of rape or incest. She may not feel prepared to take on the responsibilities of parenthood. She may feel that she hasn't enough money to raise a child or that she already has more children than she can afford. She may be afraid that a child will damage her career or that it may be born with a grave mental or physical defect, even though it has not spontaneously aborted.

A medical procedure called *amniocentesis* enables doctors to detect many possible birth defects in a fetus. Through amniocentesis, it is also possible to determine what an unborn child's sex will be. The woman—or the woman and her husband—may then want an induced abortion if the child will have a birth defect or if it promises not to be of the sex they had hoped for.

When an induced abortion is performed to protect the mother's health or life, it is known as a *therapeutic abortion*.

Induced abortions are said to be among the most frequently performed of today's surgeries. In the 1970s, it was estimated that 25 to 30 million women around the world had abortions each year. Statistics indicate that approximately 1.6 million abortions are now being performed annually in the United States. In 1980, about one-third of all pregnancies in the United States were said to be terminated by abortions. Studies show that the average woman in the Soviet Union, where birth control devices are

[9]

unpopular and difficult to obtain, has six abortions in her lifetime. In Italy, estimates hold that there may be as many as 800,000 abortions a year.

THE HEART OF
THE CONTROVERSY

A spontaneous abortion is nature's way of taking care of matters when something happens to make a birth impossible. There can be little controversy about it; people must accept it as a fact of nature when it happens. All that they can do is to provide the health and medical care that will help the mother and child avoid trouble and give them every chance of a successful birth.

But induced abortion is different. It is a human invention. As is true of many inventions, some people favor it and some oppose it; some regard it as an evil while others view it as a blessing for countless women; some want it outlawed and some want it made legal everywhere. It is induced abortion, then, that is causing today's controversy.

Actually, there is nothing new about the controversy. It has existed for as long as induced abortions have been performed—and they date back to our earliest days. There has always been controversy because induced abortion brings us up against a moral dilemma and several bewildering biological questions.

People have always looked on the murder of other human beings as morally wrong. This viewpoint leads logically to a moral concern for the fetus; if it is wrong to kill an already-born human being, it must therefore be wrong to take the life of an unborn human being. To many people, the conclusion seems a correct one. But it turns into a complex puzzle when biological questions are added, such as when can a fetus actually be called a human being and thus have the right to be protected from being killed. Is a fetus a human being from the moment of conception? Or is it simply a mass of cells that won't become human until some point later in pregnancy? If so, then it can't be murder to abort the unborn life before that point is reached, can it? But when, exactly, is that point reached? When the child begins to move within the mother's womb? When it is capable of living outside the mother even though weeks of pregnancy yet remain? Or when it is at last born?

No one knows the answers to these questions, not even biologists. But thinking people throughout the world have debated the issue for centuries and come up with various ideas and beliefs. These ideas and beliefs, differing from society to society and often in conflict with each other, have gone into the laws that govern induced abortion. We of the 1980s continue to argue the very same questions. And so there is nothing new about the controversy. What is different now is that the controversy is perhaps more heated—more angry and emotional—than ever before.

THE CONTROVERSY IN
THE UNITED STATES

In the United States, the controversy has grown because of the changes in our nation's laws on abortion. Since abortion involves the question of the cessation of life, it has always been regulated by law in all countries. For many years, the abortion laws in the United States were quite strict. They sought, as we'll see later, to protect both the mother and her unborn child by ruling that abortions were illegal except when performed to protect a woman's health and life. In recent years, however, the laws have been broadened and made more liberal. Abortions are now permitted for other reasons. Today, an American woman has the right to seek an abortion for any reason until the tenth week before the birth of her child.

Once she is within the tenth week of birth, she can be legally prevented from having an abortion. This is the law's way of handling the question of when a fetus can be judged to be a human being. The woman may still have an abortion legally, however, if her health is at stake.

We'll talk later of how today's laws came about. For now, it need only be said that such a liberal approach has triggered a nationwide argument. It should also be said that the very same controversy is taking place in many other countries where strict abortion laws of the past are now being replaced by more liberal ones.

The controversy has divided Americans into three general camps. In one are those who oppose abortion for any reason. Many of these people believe that a fetus is a human being from the moment of conception. Many other anti-abortionists feel that a fetus, even if it is not yet a human being, is still a living thing with the potential of becoming a human being. It is murder to take away the potential for life.

Holding a directly opposite view are people who believe abortion should be legal in all or almost all situations. Among these are pro-abortionists who believe that, if an abortion is performed very early, murder cannot be involved because a fetus is nothing more at that time than a collection of cells. Others say that the issue of murder never arises because they believe that a fetus is not human until the moment of birth itself. Still others seek to find a certain point during pregnancy when a fetus becomes a human being or something akin to a human being. An abortion after that point may well be murder. But even then, these pro-abortionists say, no law should be written to prevent a woman from having an abortion. The abortion concerns her body and hers alone. She—and not lawmakers—should be allowed to decide what she wants to do with her own body, letting her conscience be her guide.

Finally, there is what can be called a "middle ground" camp. It is made up of Americans who believe that abortion should be neither completely outlawed nor made completely legal. These people feel that it should be permitted only in certain instances and that an unborn life should be protected against a woman who, though perfectly capable of bearing a child and raising it, just doesn't want to have it or be burdened with raising it.

In particular, people in this camp think it wise to grant abortions in cases where there is a threat that the child will be born with a serious physical deformity or mental handicap, in cases where the woman is pregnant as a result of rape or incest, and in cases where she is clearly unfit for motherhood—perhaps too young, too emotionally unstable, or too ill for the rigors and responsibilities of raising a child. Many people also argue that abortions should be allowed only early in pregnancy when they can be most safely performed and when it is possible that the fetus has not yet become a human being.

These, then, are the three basic sides in the abortion controversy. Since they've been stated just briefly, we'll look at them in greater detail later on. There are also other arguments being voiced on the subject. We'll look at those, too.

There's nothing new about some of the above views. They're as old as the controversy itself. In fact, they're among the most basic of all the ideas and beliefs that have taken shape over the centuries as people have tried to solve the moral dilemma posed by induced abortion.

We can better understand these views as they're being expressed today if we take the time first to see how people felt about abortion in days gone by.

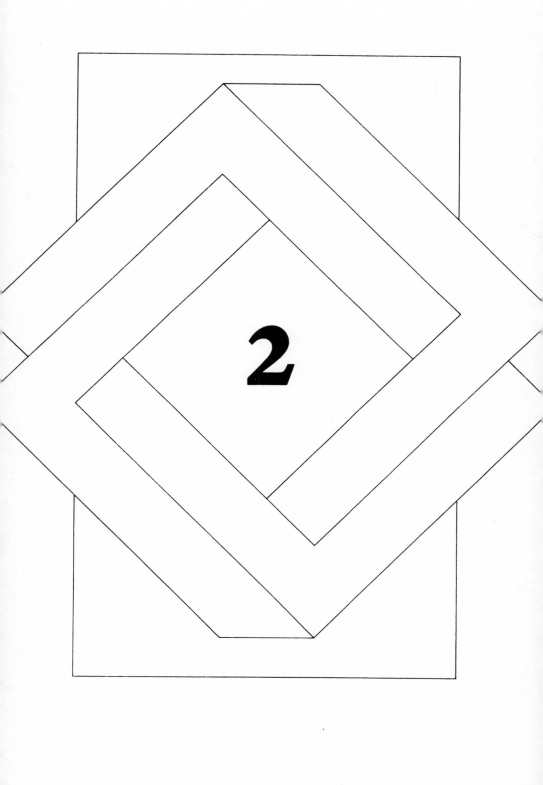

ABORTION
IN HISTORY

Induced abortions have been performed since ancient times. Historians believe a woman underwent abortions in the distant past for the same reasons that a modern woman does. Perhaps she already had a number of children and wanted no more. Perhaps she was unmarried and was ashamed to bear a child. Perhaps she was ill or felt unable to cope with the demands of birth and motherhood.

In ancient times, a woman often performed her own abortion because most societies did not know how to remove the fetus surgically or chemically. A pregnant woman might have thrust a sharp object into her uterus. She might have thrown herself from a high place or rolled along rough and stony ground. If she turned to a physician or a medicine man for help, he might have given her some foul-tasting potion to drink. Or he might have had her chant some magical prayer, asking the gods to remove the unborn child.

The feelings and attitudes of ancient peoples toward abortion were quite varied. Some societies approved of it as a means of keeping the population under control so that there would be ample food for all; some even encouraged it for this reason. Other societies opposed abortion vehemently, seeing it as murder. Some approved of it under certain circumstances.

A brief look at three early societies—Greece, Assyria, and Rome—can give us a good idea of how various ancient peoples handled the abortion problem.

THREE SOCIETIES

In Greece, abortions were permitted. Greek physicians knew how to remove the fetus through surgery or by the use of drugs. But they approached abortion with reservations, believing an unborn life was very precious. They felt that abortions should be performed only when the health of the mother was in danger. The Greek philosopher, Aristotle, looked on abortion as an efficient way to keep the population under control.

Ancient Assyria, on the other hand, was strongly opposed to abortion. Any woman who attempted to rid herself of her unborn child was guilty of a crime. The Code of Assyrian Law, believed to have been written in about 1500 B.C., called for her to be "tried, convicted, and impaled upon a stake" and to go without burial.

Abortions were permitted in ancient Rome. In fact, a Roman husband had the right to demand that his wife have an abortion if he saw fit. However, the Roman philosopher, Tertullian, viewed abortion as murder if it was performed after a fetus had developed to the point where it truly seemed to be a human being.

RELIGIOUS VIEWS

Most early religions opposed abortion. The Jewish people forbade it. The first Christians thought that it was the same as infanticide, or the killing of newborn babies. Today, the idea that abortion can be performed to safeguard the life and health of the mother is accepted in both Jewish and Protestant thought. Some religious leaders feel that there are also other acceptable grounds, such as pregnancy by rape or incest.

In its early days, the Roman Catholic Church tended to think that a fetus became a human being—was given a soul—at a certain point after conception. Abortion was permitted before that point was reached. From then on, it was seen as murder. The Church changed its view in the late nineteenth century and now assumes that a fetus is either a human being from the moment of conception or has, at that time, the potential for becoming a human at a later time. Consequently, the Church holds that a fetus may not be aborted at any age. (We'll talk at greater length of today's religious views on abortion in the next chapter.)

In Europe during the Middle Ages, the early Catholic view prevailed—that a fetus could not be aborted after a certain point. The Church warned doctors about eternal damnation for committing murder and interfering with God's handiwork.

EARLY ABORTION LAWS

As the Middle Ages came to an end, however, the abortion laws in certain countries were changed somewhat. Efforts were made to balance the health needs of the woman with the moral desire not to commit murder. The central question of when a fetus becomes a human being still remained. Early English common law attempted to solve the problem by saying that, to be legal, an abortion had to take place before *quickening*—before the fetus began to move within the mother. Quickening usually takes place about midway through pregnancy. The logic was that a fetus certainly had to be a human being once it began to move like a human being.

[19]

English common law was not alone in proclaiming quickening as the gauge for judging the start of human life. The idea was also adopted by a number of other countries and remains in use in many parts of the world today. English common law, however, was later changed to make abortion a crime throughout the entire term of a woman's pregnancy.

Much U.S. law is based on English common law. Our first state laws called abortion a crime only if performed after quickening. Then, in the latter half of the nineteenth century, as had happened to English common law, the laws were altered. Abortion was made a crime at any time. This was done mainly to protect women against the patent medicines of the day.

These medicines were concoctions that were said to relieve all types of illness. Among them were potions meant to help women abort. Most patent medicines were useless and many, containing generous amounts of opium, were seen as dangerous avenues to drug addiction. They were nevertheless widely used because, laced with opium as they were, they did relieve pain, and people felt that there was nothing else to which they could turn for help. Medical science still had much to learn about alleviating pain and curing illness.

Though the U.S. laws against abortion were strictly worded, they did not call for the harshest of penalties. Violators were not punished as murderers. A physician who performed an abortion was guilty of a felony and could be imprisoned and fined, but was not tried for homicide unless the mother died as a result of the abortion. Women were usually not even prosecuted.

Then a number of states held that abortion was legal so long as it was performed to safeguard the mother's health and so long as it was performed within the first three months of pregnancy. This view prevailed throughout much of the country until the 1960s. At that time, things began to change.

THE WINDS OF CHANGE

The changes did not originate in the United States, however. They were first seen in Europe. There, abortion for purposes of protecting the mother's health had become legal in many countries. But now several nations took steps to liberalize their laws and declare abortion legal for other reasons.

Several factors brought about the changes. For one, thanks to modern medicine, abortions could now be performed more safely than ever before. For another, people began to feel that there were other reasons for abortion that were just as compelling and valid as the mother's health. Why, the question was asked, should a woman be made to bear a child who promised to be seriously deformed? Why should she be made to bear an unwanted child who had been conceived during rape or incest? Why should she be made to bear a child if it was clear that she was unfit for motherhood? It was felt that everyone would suffer in these cases—the woman, her family, the child itself, and the state. The child might well be neglected by the mother. If a child needed special medical care that would cripple the family financially, the state would have to provide some or all of the child's support.

There was also a growing feeling that the law should not tell a woman what she could or could not do with her own body; the decision should be left to her. And there was concern that the world was becoming over-populated. As Aristotle had felt centuries earlier, abortion promised to be a highly efficient means of keeping the planet from becoming too crowded.

There was yet another reason for liberalizing abortion laws and it was among the most important. People felt that a woman who really wanted an abortion wouldn't be stopped by any set of laws. If she was desperate enough, she would get one anyway. This posed a serious health danger.

Most reputable physicians would not run the risk of performing an illegal operation. A pregnant woman was forced to turn elsewhere for help. She was forced to go to doctors who had lost their licenses or their professional standing because of alcoholism, drug abuse, or some other serious reason. Or, worse, she was forced to seek out someone who was untrained in medicine but nevertheless willing to cash in on her problem.

Further, few hospitals would risk their reputations by admitting women for abortions. Though some abortionists ran clean and well-equipped clinics, a woman usually had to make her way to some hideaway for the illegal operation. It might be an apartment, a garage, a concealed spot in a warehouse, or a cubbyhole at the back of a store. Frequently, the place was located in the worst of neighborhoods. It was never up to hospital standards of cleanliness, and women were threatened with the possibility of infection.

If not acquainted with the ways of the underworld, the woman did not know where to find an abortionist. Often she was not able to afford the fee and was then forced to abort herself. Imitating women of early times, she thrust sticks and needles—even coat hangers—into herself. She could suffer tragic consequences.

There is no way to compile a record of secret operations and so no one knows how many women lost their lives, were seriously injured, or made desperately ill because of illegal abortions. But, worldwide, the number was estimated to be in the millions. (Some idea of the loss of life can be had by looking at Italy today, where abortions are legal in a fairly wide variety of cases. Despite the nation's liberal laws, some 600,000 illegal abortions are performed there annually. They result in 2,000 to 2,500 deaths. There are about 200,000 legal abortions in Italy per year.)

Something had to be done to change the laws. The first changes were seen in the Scandinavian countries. There, it was decided that abortions could be performed for reasons that included a mother's health and the danger that her child would be born defective. The changes then spread to other nations. In the fifteen years between 1966 and 1981, seventeen countries liberalized their abortion laws to some degree; among them were Canada, Great Britain, India, Japan, and Russia. In Russia and Japan, for instance, abortion came to be permitted for a wide variety of reasons if the operation was performed by a qualified doctor and (usually) within the first trimester. In 1968, Great Britain made abortion legal under certain conditions. Two doctors had to agree that an abortion was necessary. It was seen as necessary if the mother's mental or physical health was at stake, if the well-being of her other children seemed threatened, or if the fetus showed serious abnormalities.

Today, abortion laws vary greatly among the world's nations. Some now permit abortion on request for any reason. Some allow it for specific reasons only. Some countries recognize just one or two reasons while others recognize several; the reasons range from the traditional one of the mother's health to economic hardship. Seven countries—Bulgaria, Czechoslovakia, Hungary, Rumania, Iran, Israel, and New Zealand—have moved against the trend toward liberalization and have actually toughened their abortion laws since the mid-1960s. Abortion continues to be prohibited in countries where Roman Catholicism is the principal religion, though some permit it to save the mother's life; they include Spain and all the Latin American countries except Cuba. It is also prohibited in most countries of the Moslem faith.

In addition to Cuba, there is a major exception among the predominantly Catholic nations. As mentioned earlier, Italy has a liberal abortion law on the books. Enacted in 1978, the law allows any woman eighteen years or older to ask for an abortion within the first ninety days of pregnancy. At that time, she may have an abortion if her physical or mental health is endangered, if the pregnancy is the result of rape, or if the fetus is malformed. An abortion may also be granted for such socioeconomic reasons as personal or financial inability to raise the child.

In 1981, the nation's Catholic political leaders put a measure on the ballot to limit severely the scope of the law. They asked that abortions be granted only when the mother's health is in jeopardy. The measure was defeated by a margin of between 68 and 70 percent.

CHANGES IN AMERICAN ABORTION LAWS

As was happening elsewhere, the attitude of many Americans toward abortion was changing in the 1950s and 1960s—and for the same reasons. There was a growing call for the states to liberalize their laws.

In 1959, the American Law Institute developed a set of guidelines that the states could follow in making their changes. In its Model Penal Code, the Institute proposed that pregnancies could be terminated for the following reasons: (1) health, (2) the risk that the child would be born with a serious mental or physical abnormality, and (3) pregnancy due to rape, incest, or other "felonious intercourse." Felonious intercourse included all illicit sexual relations with girls under sixteen years of age.

Eight years later, in 1967, Colorado became the first state to liberalize its abortion laws in line with the American Law Institute's proposals. In the next years, a number of other states followed suit, among them California, Hawaii, Alaska, and Wisconsin. They were joined by the District of Columbia. All of them permitted abortions for a variety of reasons other than the health of the mother.

Most states, however, continued to keep their strict laws of old on the books. Then, in 1973, the United States Supreme Court issued a ruling that forced them to change.

The Court said that the ruling was based on the Fourteenth Amendment to the Constitution or, specifically, on "the Fourteenth Amendment's concept of personal liberty and restrictions upon state action." The ruling held that no state could prevent a woman from having an abortion within the first six months of pregnancy. Only in the last ten weeks of pregnancy could a state forbid the operation. By that time, the child was known to be *viable*—capable of living outside the mother—and thus assuredly a human being and entitled to have its life protected. But, even then, the state could not prevent an abortion if the mother's health was in jeopardy.

The Supreme Court decision made abortion legal throughout the land. It affected all states with strict abortion laws. The decision was applauded by pro-abortionists and condemned by anti-abortionists. The controversy, which had been building for years as abortion laws were being liberalized throughout the world, now burst into full flower here in the United States.

The next years saw organized pro- and anti-abortion groups demonstrate in meetings and on the streets. The years also saw anti-abortionist legislators in Congress propose laws that would sidestep the Court's ruling.

At the same time, Congress and the states began allocating funds to help the poor pay for abortions. This was done because many legislators realized that well-to-do women could easily afford to go to a reputable doctor or hospital for their abortions but that countless poor women would be forced to seek out cheaper abortions elsewhere or would still be forced to abort themselves. However, many people thought it criminal for any government—federal or state—to provide monies meant to take the lives of innocent unborn children.

Today, the controversy continues to rage more fiercely than ever. In a later chapter, we'll talk more of what's being said and done at present. But now let's return to the principal arguments for and against abortion. We've looked at some briefly. We now have to look at them—and a number of others—more closely so that you can begin to decide where you'll want to stand in the controversy facing us as individuals and as citizens.

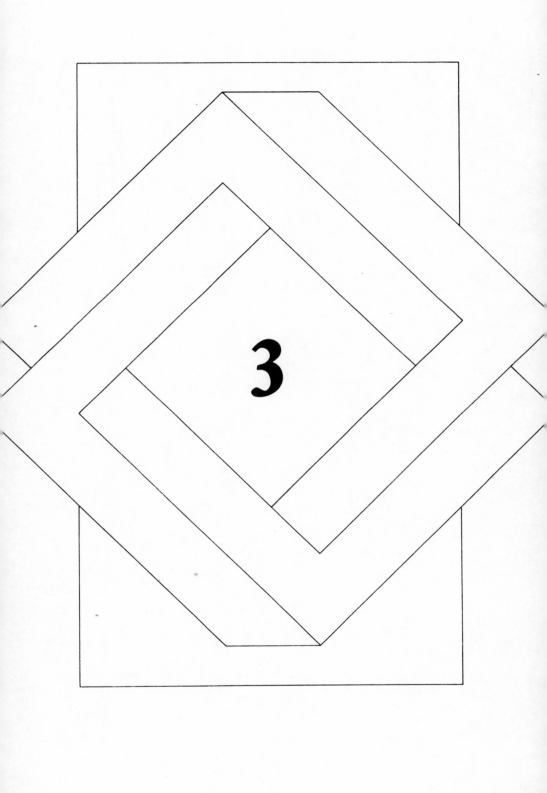

ABORTION AND ITS QUESTIONS

Let's begin looking at the pros and cons of the abortion controversy with that most basic and puzzling of questions: when does human life actually begin?

For many people, this is the central question in the discussion. If the point at which the fetus reaches humanness could be conclusively established, they feel that the controversy could be settled logically. Abortion would not be wrong before the point of humanness. It should be outlawed after that point.

But there is a problem here. As has been stressed before, no one has been able to answer the question with finality. Those thinkers who looked into it in centuries past all came up with views that were based on personal and religious beliefs and not on scientifically discovered information. There just weren't enough facts to work with. And so the views were many and varied, ranging from humanness beginning at conception to humanness beginning at birth.

Modern scientists are in much the same position as the thinkers of old. They have, of course, more solid information on the development of the fetus than ever before, but still not enough for any definite conclusions. Their thinking is based on a combination of what they've seen, how they've responded to their observations, and what they personally believe.

For instance, some scientists contend that human life must begin at conception. They point to a fact that is now beyond dispute—that biological life commences when the mother's egg is united with the father's sperm. These scientists feel that the fertilized egg is not only biological life but also human life. It is something more than a collection of cells. It is a unique genetic entity, quite distinct from all others. It is the product of two human beings. Hence, it also must be human.

On the other hand, there are scientists who believe that human life does not begin until a week or so after conception. By this time, the fertilized egg has traveled through the fallopian tubes (where fertilization took place) to the uterus and has implanted itself in the wall there. The embryo can be seen taking shape. The beginnings of activity can be discerned. This assuredly must be human life. If it isn't, one scientist asks, then what is?

But it isn't life yet, in the view of still other scientists. Some of their number argue that humanness doesn't occur until the embryo's heart begins to beat—in about the fourth week of pregnancy. And many others say that humanness arrives sometime between the sixth and eighth week of pregnancy.

By the sixth week, the nervous sytem has developed to the point where simple reflexes can be noted. By the eighth week, the embryo is developing into a fetus. Hands, arms, legs, and the internal organs are taking shape. Thus, many scientists say that the fetus must be judged to have become a human being.

But there are still further views. One holds that humanness arrives with quickening, which takes place about midway through a pregnancy. Another view opts for

[30]

an even later date, the time when the fetus becomes viable. As you know, a fetus is said to be viable when it is able to live outside the mother. Viability is customarily seen as sometime during the twenty-fourth to twenty-eighth week.

The Supreme Court's 1973 decision, ruling that no state may outlaw abortion until the tenth week before birth, is based on the concept of humanness at viability. A problem has arisen in the wake of the decision, however. The time of viability has changed since 1973. Doctors have been able to remove and keep alive some fetuses that are only twenty weeks old.

And so there are many shades of scientific opinion on when human life begins in the fetus. Anti-abortionists agree with those scientists who argue for humanness at conception or very shortly thereafter. Pro-abortionists agree with the later dates or feel that the whole idea of the beginning of humanness should be disregarded and attention given to other factors favoring abortion. In all cases, personal and moral opinions are being considered in place of scientific fact. It is simply not yet known when human life begins. And, the life process being as mysterious and complex as it is, we may never know when life begins, no matter how far science advances in the future.

By itself, then, science can be of little help in the abortion controversy. Scientists can do no more than provide some biological information. Armed with that information, people are left to decide for themselves when it seems reasonable to say that humanness begins and to decide what must be done about abortion at that point. For guidance in their decision, many people have turned to their churches.

WHERE DO THE CHURCHES STAND?

The world's organized religions hold a variety of views on the morality of abortion and the circumstances under which it may or may not be permitted.

Among the strictest abortion views held today are those of the Roman Catholic Church. As you know from chapter 2, in its earliest years the Church held the view that humanness did not come—that God did not breathe a soul into a child—until some point after conception. Abortion was permitted up to that point. The point itself was set at forty days after conception for males and eighty days after conception for females, with abortion being permissible before these times. This concept came in part from the Greek philosopher, Aristotle. He got the idea from his various beliefs about the soul and from his studies of the growth of animal eggs and the first movements of the human fetus; it is also reflective of the old belief that the male was the stronger and more important of the two sexes. The idea was without any scientific foundation, but it pretty much prevailed in the world and the Church until the latter half of the nineteenth century.

At that time, a number of Catholic thinkers began to argue that God breathed a soul into an unborn child at a much earlier date, perhaps at conception, perhaps just a few days afterward. Of course, no one could pinpoint the exact time. And so the Church took the stand that a child was either a human being at conception or had the potential of soon becoming human. That potential was judged to be quite as important as humanness itself. An unborn child, then, had to be protected from abortion right from conception.

This view was strengthened in 1930 when Pope Pius XI issued his encyclical (a letter to the church membership) entitled *Casti Connubii*. In it, the Pope called abortion "a very serious crime" and stated that, from conception, there was no justifiable reason for "the direct killing of the innocent" unborn child. This meant that socioeconomic factors and even the mother's health could not be used as grounds for abortion. Later pontiffs, including Paul VI and the present Pope John Paul II, have stated these same views.

The words *direct killing* in the encyclical are important. While the Catholic Church sees the direct killing of a fetus as a moral wrong, it does not oppose what it calls indirect killing. Indirect killing refers to the coincidental death of a fetus when medication or medical help is given to the mother to save her life. Perhaps desperately ill, she may require a drug or treatment that, though it is not specifically intended to do so, kills the fetus. Or perhaps she is suffering from a cancer of the reproductive organs, with the result that they must be removed and the fetus lost. The Church sees these as tragic incidents but not as sinful acts.

In the minds of many Catholic thinkers, the indirect killing exception puts the Church right next door to permitting therapeutic abortions. They feel that the Church should broaden its views to allow abortions to save a mother's life.

The Church's very strong stand against abortion is accompanied by a serious penalty for Catholics who ignore it. The Catholic Bishops of the United States issued a message for the parishes of the nation soon after the Supreme Court's 1973 decision. They warned all American Catholics that anyone who underwent or performed an abortion was subject to excommunication. Excommunication means dismissal from the Church.

In the Protestant and Jewish faiths, opinions on abortion range from strong "anti" feelings to equally strong "pro" sentiments. All Protestant denominations and all the Jewish groups—Orthodox, Conservative, and Reformed— see abortion as a serious moral problem. Many of them oppose it outright, either from conception or from very early in pregnancy.

In general, however, most Protestant denominations and Jewish groups think that abortions can be performed, both legally and morally, under certain circumstances. For instance, the Mormon Church brands abortion as a "revolting and sinful practice," but feels that it should be allowed when physicians agree that it is necessary to save a mother's "seriously endangered" life. Mormon belief also holds that abortion is permissible when the pregnancy is "caused by rape and produces serious emotional trauma in the mother."

The Lutheran Church-Missouri Synod agrees that abortions should be performed for a mother's health. The Synod, however, draws the line at economic and psychiatric reasons and states that, by themselves, they are not justifiable grounds for abortion.

When an Orthodox rabbi recently testified before a congressional subcommittee studying some proposed abortion measures, he said that Judaism has always sanctioned abortion for a mother's physical health "in at least limited circumstances." He added that some Jewish authorities have also permitted abortions to preserve the mother's sanity.

Many Protestant denominations and Jewish groups do not feel that the humanness of a fetus should be the central issue in deciding when an abortion is right or wrong. They believe, rather, that the entire picture of the woman's life, the family's life, and the unborn child's future life should be taken into consideration. Various factors—such as what will happen to the quality of life for the woman and the child because the birth is not wanted—should all be weighed before a decision is made.

For instance, suppose the child will be born with a serious deformity that will keep it and the family from living a full, happy, and productive life. Or suppose that the woman's life will be made so unbearable by an unwanted child that she will become physically or mentally ill and perhaps cause the family to break up. Or suppose that the unwanted child will be physically mistreated, even killed, or abandoned and left to be raised in public institutions. In the view of many Protestant and Jewish thinkers, if these and other possibilities exist, it would be a moral act, perhaps even a loving act, to terminate the pregnancy.

In addition, much Protestant and Jewish thought holds that only the people most directly involved with a pregnancy are the ones really able to judge whether an abortion is necessary or justified. They are the mother, the

[34]

father, the family, and the doctor. They—and especially the mother—should always have the final say in deciding whether to abort or not.

As a case in point, take the possibility that they are faced with a birth that will produce a mentally or physically defective child. While certain prenatal tests—among them amniocentesis, which was mentioned in chapter 1—can indicate the presence of a defect, many cannot determine the degree of that defect. Is it then ethical to abort a child with Down's syndrome, a form of mental retardation that could be mild or very serious? Or ethical to abort in the presence of the genetically-determined Tay-Sachs disease? It leads to a painful death within a few years, and the raising of such an afflicted child for those few years constitutes a terrible emotional and economic burden for the family. So, in cases such as these, who is best able to decide whether to abort or not? In the eyes of many Jewish and Protestant thinkers, only the mother and the people closest to her, especially the father. Only they, and not a lawmaker, can know whether they have the stamina, the patience, and the ability to do a good job of raising the child, and whether they will be able to stand the economic and financial strain involved. There should be no laws to prevent them from reaching the decision that, in the light of all the circumstances, they believe is the right one.

Most press coverage of abortion concentrates on the mother and rarely mentions the father. But some points about his role in the abortion decision must now be mentioned. First, there is nothing in the Supreme Court's 1973 ruling that gives the father the right to stop the mother from having an abortion. Nor is there any federal or state law that requires the mother to have the father's consent before an abortion can be performed. In several states, however, a wife is required to inform the husband that she intends to get an abortion. Secondly, it is now thought that an abortion can be as emotionally traumatic an experience for the man as for the woman. Studies show that he knows little about the operation, that he fears the mother will be injured, and that he wants to do what is best for her. To help him through his own emotional upset and to help him better understand the problems of the woman, counseling programs for the man have been established in three northern California areas—in San Francisco and in Alameda and Contra Costa counties. Sponsored by the local Planned Parenthood associations, the programs are reportedly the first of their kind in the nation. It is hoped that similar programs will be established elsewhere.

WHO SHALL DECIDE?

We come now to one of the most hotly debated issues in the controversy: who has the right to decide whether or not there shall be an abortion—the law or the individual?

Anti-abortionists point out that an unborn child cannot defend itself against being killed. There is, then, only one way to protect it. There must be strong laws against aborting after the time that a child can be said to be a human being and thus to hold the rights of a human being. Anti-abortionists, as we have seen, tend to set the time of humanness at conception or at implantation a few days later. From then on, in their view, there can be no individual decision on abortion.

Anti-abortionists fear that the mother, by herself or with the help of those around her, will decide to have an abortion for purely selfish reasons that have nothing to do with danger to her health or life. Perhaps she'll not want a child because it promises to destroy the plans she has for her life. Actions such as these will deprive the child of a life many people believe it has a right to have.

To justify their fears, anti-abortionists point to some recent statistics. Prior to the 1973 Supreme Court decision, there were 744,600 legal abortions in the country—legal because they were protecting the mother's health. Since 1973, the annual U.S. abortion total has jumped to around 1.6 million. Certainly, the anti-abortion argument holds, not all these surgeries have been performed for therapeutic reasons. "Selfish" motives have assuredly been behind many.

The anti-abortion view was briefly summed up by Republican Representative Henry J. Hyde of Illinois in a 1981 interview in the magazine *U.S. News & World Report*. When asked why he favors outlawing abortion, Representative Hyde replied:

"Because abortion is the killing of an innocently inconvenient human life. If human life is precious in our society, it ought to be protected from extermination, whether for sociological, economical, or any other reasons. We legally protect snail darters, wild birds, and dolphins—even lawn grass. The unborn child is particularly vulnerable and needs protection."

Then, on being asked if a woman should be allowed to decide for herself on whether to have an abortion, Mr. Hyde said:

"No. Neither a woman nor a man should have the right to kill another human being. The fetus or embryo in the woman is a separate human being with its own blood-circulation system and brain waves."

Representative Hyde is one of the many anti-abortionists who believe that humanness takes place at conception. He is the coauthor of a proposed anti-abortion bill in Congress. We'll talk more about the bill in the next chapter.

On the opposite side of the fence, pro-abortionists feel that the mother—perhaps helped by the father, her family, and her doctor—should have the final decision on an abortion. It is her body—and hers alone—that is involved. They feel that lawmakers have no right to tell her what to do with that body.

They argue that those who want to make the laws don't know what an unwanted child will do to her life. Nor are the lawmakers the ones who will have to raise the child. They're not the ones who will have their lives changed by the child. So what right do they have to make such a critical decision for the mother? She's the only one with the right because she's the one with the problem.

But many pro-abortionists recognize that an unborn child has a right to live. Consequently, many feel that a time limit should be set on the right of the mother to decide. In the minds of most, the limit is best set at the time of viability—that point when a child is at last capable of surviving on its own outside the mother. Karen Mulhauser, the executive director of the National Abortion Rights League, is among those who agree with the viability limit. Speaking in opposition to Representative Hyde in the *U.S. News & World Report* interview, she said:

"Only then [at viability] should the rights of the fetus be balanced against the rights of the woman. And, even then, abortion is allowed [in the Supreme Court's 1973 ruling] to protect a woman's life or health." About aborting earlier in pregnancy, she remarked, "We should never put the rights of an embryo or a fertilized egg above the rights of a pregnant woman."

But what if, even though there is as yet no scientific proof of it, the anti-abortionists are right in their belief that humanness comes much earlier than viability, perhaps as early as conception? The woman who aborts early is then killing—murdering—a human being. Shouldn't she be stopped by law?

Pro-abortionists reply that, even then the woman should still be the one to decide whether or not to abort. Just as she is the one who must live with the unwanted child, so is she the one who must live with her conscience and suffer whatever it tells her. If she believes in God, then she is the one who must live in fear of how she will be judged.

As was said earlier, much Protestant and Jewish thought agrees that it is the woman's right to decide because she is the one most directly involved in the situation. The hope here is that, perhaps assisted by the loved ones around her, she will look at all the factors and then make her decision on the basis of those factors, her conscience, and her sense of responsibility.

Among the Protestant churches supporting this view is the United Presbyterian Church in the United States of America. In 1972, it stated that "women should have full freedom of personal choice concerning the completion or termination of their pregnancies . . . the artificial or induced termination of pregnancy, therefore, should not be restricted by law."

Similar views have been expressed by such churches as the United Christian Church, the Reformed Church, The American Baptist Churches in the United States of America, and the Episcopal Church. A statement in 1973 by the Episcopal Church called for the removal of abortion laws so that there could be a "free and responsible exercise of Christian conscience" in the making of abortion decisions. In the opinion of all these churches, as well as many Jewish groups, the decision to abort or not to abort should be a matter of personal conscience, with the individuals involved always seeking to make the most responsible decision possible.

ABORTION AND IMMORALITY

Some anti-abortionists argue that strong abortion laws are needed not just because abortion is, in itself, immoral, but because it also promotes immorality. Adults and young people, they say, become sexually promiscuous if they know there is an easy and legal way to get an abortion should the woman become pregnant.

As proof of what they say, the anti-abortionists again point to the growing number of abortions in the country—up from 744,600 in 1973 to an estimated 1.6 million in 1980. They also point out that, in 1980, more than a million American teenagers became pregnant and that 38 percent of them had abortions.

This view is seen as groundless by pro-abortionists. They argue that there may have been just as many abortions prior to 1973, but that we don't know about them because they were illegal and went unreported. It can't be said for certain that there are appreciably more actual abortions today than before. All that can be said is that, because abortion is legal, more are reported and accounted for in the nation's statistics.

It is further argued by pro-abortionists that no one has been able to establish any sort of relationship between the availability of legal abortions and a decline in a country's morality. If there is indeed such a decline, then other factors may be responsible or may at least be partly responsible—factors such as the breakdown of the family and the problem of growing violence in the country.

Pro-abortionists feel that the anti-abortion laws themselves are immoral. First, they say that the laws turn an innocent woman into a criminal by forcing her to break the laws when abortion seems to be the only reasonable solution to her problem. Second, as Karen Mulhauser argued in the *U.S. News & World Report* interview:

". . . it is immoral to force a twelve-year-old victim of incest to continue a pregnancy and, as a child, to raise a child. It is immoral to force a couple who knows that the woman is carrying a seriously deformed fetus to bring that child into the world. Also, it is immoral to force any woman who is unwillingly pregnant and in desperate need of medical care to continue her pregnancy."

Finally, there is the argument that the laws are immoral because they force the woman into dangerous situations when, in desperation, she seeks an abortion. As you'll recall from chapter 2, she is forced to turn to someone willing to break the law for the money to be had in performing an illegal operation—perhaps a doctor who has lost his or her standing in the medical profession, perhaps someone who is medically untrained. Untrained people are a particular menace and are to be found in great number in the area of illegal abortions; a survey of a small American city once showed that the abortionists there included an antique dealer and a mechanic. A woman is often forced to go to "operating rooms" hidden away in the worst part of town. If she cannot find an abortionist, or if she can't afford the operation, she may try to abort herself by thrusting sticks or pins or even coat hangers into her body, and the dangers to her health and even her life are terrible. Pro-abortionists view laws that enable a woman to get a legal abortion in a reputable hospital, with a reputable doctor in charge, as being far more moral than laws that might force her to take grave risks.

WHAT ABOUT ADOPTION?

Adoption is the court procedure that enables a child born of one set of parents to become, legally, the child of someone else. Most often, children are adopted by couples. But it is also possible for just one person to adopt a child. For example, a woman's second husband may adopt the child—or children—of her first marriage.

Many anti-abortionists view adoption as one of the most solid arguments in favor of their cause. It makes no sense, they say, to kill an unborn child when, on its birth, it can be placed for adoption. Everyone then benefits. The biological mother is no longer burdened with an unwanted child. A couple that yearns for a child is given one. And the child is allowed the gift of life and raised with loving care.

Pro-abortionists reply that this might well be a solution—but only in those cases where the mother is willing to bear the child so that it can then be placed with another couple. But she should not be forced to endure a pregnancy—or take risks with her health if the pregnancy is a difficult one—just because there happens to be such a thing as adoption. The choice of whether to have the child or an abortion should still be hers.

The pro-abortionists also see possible problems for the biological mother in adoption. To understand these problems, we have to know something of the adoption laws in the United States. In their details, the adoption laws vary among the states, but the following points prevail throughout the country. First, a child cannot be placed for adoption without the consent of the biological parents unless they: (1) are underage, (2) are mentally incompetent, (3) have abandoned the youngster, or (4) have lost custody to it through neglectful or cruel treatment. Second, if the child is born of unmarried parents (and statistics show that most adopted children are), then only the biological mother's consent is necessary. In most states, the natural parents' consent is required if they are fourteen years or older.

These laws are fine, the pro-abortionists agree, and are there for the protection of the biological parent. But what if the mother is unmarried and so young—even at fourteen or so—that she can be easily influenced by her parents? Suppose they argue that she should keep the child because "it's the right thing to do" or because they've come to love the newborn infant. She may give in and, against her real feelings, burden herself for years with a child that she doesn't want to raise and perhaps isn't mature enough to raise. It's a situation that could ruin her life.

Next, the nation's adoption laws call for the biological parents to give up all rights to the child upon adoption. They don't know who adopts the child or where the child is to live. The child, on being adopted, is even provided with a new birth certificate.

Again, the pro-abortionists agree that these are sound laws, this time designed to protect adopted children and their adoptive parents from ever meeting the birth parents. Children, if they know they're adopted, might not want to see the biological parents who "gave them away." The adoptive parents might not want to be put in the position of telling the youngster that he or she is adopted. But it often happens that the birth mother (or father) grows curious about the child, wonders what the child looks like, and wonders how he or she is growing and faring. All these thoughts can be a terrible burden to bear. The mother may, as a number of women have done before her, attempt to locate her child. It can be a heartbreaking search that will usually end in frustration because the authorities are careful to protect the privacy of the child and the adoptive parents.

And pro-abortionists see further difficulties—difficulties that concern the child and the state. In practically all areas of the country, adoptions are usually handled by public or private agencies that are licensed by the state. Before going to court to have an adoption made final, these agencies take great pains to "match" a child with adoptive parents so far as background and even physical characteristics are concerned (some states require that the child and the adoptive parents be of the same religion). But statistics show that the agencies sometimes have trouble placing certain children for adoption. "Cuddly" infants and good-looking children are usually easily placed. Not so easy to place are older children, children with physical or mental handicaps, children from various minority groups, and children who are not physically attractive. They may have to live out their young lives in institutions. Institutional life can be difficult, and it can constitute a very heavy financial burden for the state to bear.

And so, to return to their basic view, pro-abortionists feel that the decision to abort or to bear a child should be left with the woman or with the woman and her husband if she is married. Adoption should not be used as a reason for passing a law outlawing abortion.

WILL ABORTION
LAWS WORK?

Here, we turn from questions of science, morality, and adoption to another kind of question. It is a very practical one. Will abortion laws work and actually stop women from having abortions?

The question is not only a practical one, but also a somewhat difficult one for anti-abortionists to answer. There is much evidence to show that a woman who desperately wants an abortion will not be stopped simply because it is illegal.

[43]

Realistically, anti-abortionists must admit that all women won't be stopped. Further, no law has ever kept *all* people from committing crimes.

What the anti-abortionists hope is that at least some women will be stopped and that many unborn lives will thus be saved. Again, anti-abortionists point to the statistics showing the increase in abortions between 1973 and 1980. They argue that, if U.S. law was returned to its pre-1973 stance, the abortion rate might drop to where it was then. Close to three-quarters of a million unborn babies would be spared each year. Some people feel it is possible to save even more lives if the pre-1973 practice of allowing abortions for the mother's health was also eliminated.

Pro-abortionists state flatly that no law will stop a woman if she is desperate enough. As proof, they point not only to the number of illegal abortions of times past but also to the experiences of countries that today have strict laws on their books.

For instance, Belgium allows abortions only to save the mother's life or health. It is known that thousands of Belgian women yearly get around this law by traveling just a few miles and crossing into the Netherlands. There, legal abortions are more easily obtained.

Another example: A New Zealand woman may obtain an abortion for the sake of her physical or mental health. In 1977, however, anti-abortionists there succeeded in passing a law that called for all requested abortions to be reviewed by medical experts to determine if the physical or mental danger was sufficient to warrant the operation. The review was a lengthy and cumbersome one and was obviously meant to discourage women from requesting abortions.

Immediately after passage of the law, the New Zealand abortion rate dropped by 3,000 per year—because women flew to Australia for legal abortions. Since then, the rate has gone up to about 4,000 annually, chiefly, it is reported, because women are learning how to present the proper psychological symptoms to the review board.

[44]

Still another example: As do so many predominantly Catholic nations, Brazil forbids abortion for any reason. A highly lucrative "illegal abortion industry" has taken shape there. It has become so large that the country is trying to combat it by introducing a nationwide family planning program.

And, finally, the pro-abortionists point to Italy, a Catholic country that has nevertheless developed a very liberal abortion law (to refresh your memory on the law, see page 23, chapter 2). The law doesn't cover all women, however, with the result that there are an estimated 600,000 illegal abortions in Italy each year.

And so the questions and answers concerning the controversy are many. The problem is that most of the questions simply cannot be answered with indisputable fact. People have been forced to decide where they stand on the basis of their personal opinion and their personal views of morality, perhaps guided by the thinking of those around them or by their religious beliefs. It is the "unanswerable" quality of the controversy that has helped to make it as heated and emotional as it is today.

The abortion controversy is also especially heated today because it has become a political issue. It is to the politics of abortion that we turn next.

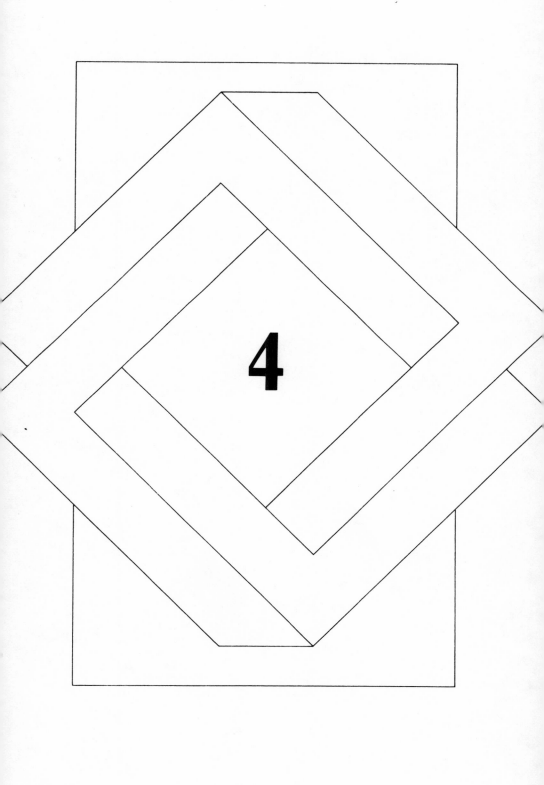

ABORTION AND POLITICS

Until 1973, the federal government played little or no part in the development of abortion laws in the United States. As was true in many other issues, each state was free to develop its own laws as it saw fit. Then the case of *Roe* v. *Wade* came before the U.S. Supreme Court for a decision.

ROE v. WADE

The case involved the abortion laws in Texas and Georgia. Texas permitted abortion only to protect a mother's health. Georgia allowed abortions to protect the mother's health, in instances of rape, and when a fetus might be deformed. These laws were being challenged by pregnant women seeking abortions.

In essence, the case asked if a state had the constitutional right, under Section 1 of the Fourteenth Amendment, to make laws that interfered with a woman's right to have an abortion. Were not such laws a violation of her privacy? Section 1 of the Fourteenth Amendment reads:

> All persons born or naturalized in the United States, and subject to the jurisdiction thereof, are citizens of the United States and the State wherein they reside. No State shall make or enforce any law which shall abridge the privileges or immunities of citizens of the United States; nor shall any State deprive any person of life, liberty, or property, without due process of law; nor deny to any person within its jurisdiction the equal protection of the laws.

The Court came out in favor of a woman's right to choose freely to have an abortion. By a 7–2 margin, the Court ruled that a woman holds the constitutional right to an abortion during at least the first six months of pregnancy. Only when she is within ten weeks of birth—when the child is viable—can the state outlaw abortion. At that time, however, abortions remain permissible if the mother's life or health is at stake.

The majority opinion of the Court was written by Justice Harry Blackmun. In that opinion, he wrote that the ruling was based on "the Fourteenth Amendment's concept of personal liberty and restrictions upon state action." Justice Blackmun said that the Amendment guaranteed a privacy right that included "a woman's decision whether or not to terminate her pregnancy."

Texas and Georgia had argued that a fetus was a "person" and thus was also entitled to "equal protection under the laws" as stated in the Amendment. The Court, Justice Blackmun wrote, rejected this argument and put the woman's rights ahead of those of the fetus.

However, the Court also recognized the rights of the unborn child. These rights came into play in the tenth week before birth. Justice Blackmun wrote that, in those weeks, a "state may go so far as to proscribe abortion" because the fetus by then "presumably has capability of a meaningful life outside the mother's womb."

Note Jusice Blackmun's careful wording here. He says that a state *may* (not *should* or *must*) outlaw abortion and that the fetus is *presumably* (meaning *assumed, not conclusively known*) able to live outside the mother. Though these are indefinite terms, they must be used here. In effect, for constitutional purposes, the ruling sets viability as the beginning of humanness because it seems reasonable to assume that human life has certainly started by this time. But the Court is in the same boat with the rest of us; it doesn't know for certain when humanness actually begins. And so it can do no more than say that a state, if its conscience so dictates, may prohibit abortion at viability because the fetus may be a human being at that time and thus entitled to have its life protected under the Constitution.

Though the Court put the woman's rights first until the tenth week before birth, it must be pointed out that the Justices did not give her the *sole* say in abortion matters prior to that time.

Justice Blackmun wrote that, even if a state could not bar abortion in the first six months, it had the right to take certain actions in the fourth, fifth, and sixth months. It could, he wrote, "properly assert important interest in safeguarding health, in maintaining medical standards, and in protecting potential life." This meant that a state had the right to pass regulations concerning who could perform abortions, where they could be performed, and the standards that would have to be observed in performing them. Remember also that abortions could be performed in the final ten weeks before birth if the mother's health or life was in jeopardy.

AFTER THE DECISION

The decision, which was announced on January 22, 1973, caused an uproar. Abortion, at least during the first six

[51]

months of pregnancy, became legal throughout the land. The strict Texas and Georgia laws were not the only ones overturned by the decision; the laws in forty-four other states were likewise toppled. (At the time, as was mentioned in chapter 2, only a handful of states had opted for liberal abortion laws, among them Alaska, California, Colorado, Hawaii, and Wisconsin, plus the District of Columbia.)

Pro-abortionists, who preferred to be called "pro-choice" advocates because they believed it was the woman's right to choose abortion, were jubilant. They had been urging liberal laws since the 1950s and 1960s. Now they had won a great victory. In fact, with abortion now legalized nationally, many of their number thought the controversy had been settled for good.

It didn't take the pro-choice supporters long to realize how mistaken they were. Millions of people—from political leaders to ordinary citizens—were appalled by the Court's decision. They immediately condemned it, both in word and action. The decision had not ended the controversy. The reverse was true. The controversy had been growing for years and now was about to explode.

Among those who took immediate action was Republican Senator James L. Buckley of New York. He sought to sidestep the ruling by introducing in Congress a Constitutional amendment that would prohibit all abortions except those meant to save the mother's life. His bill was cosponsored by five fellow Republicans—Senators Mark Hatfield of Oregon, Wallace F. Bennett of Utah, Carl T. Curtis of Nebraska, Milton R. Young of North Dakota, and Dewey F. Bartlett of Oklahoma.

The proposed amendment also attacked the Court's opinion that abortions be prohibited only after viability. The amendment defined human life as starting when the fertilized egg implants itself in the uterus sometime between five and seven days after conception. Under the amendment's definition, any abortive technique used after this brief period would be illegal unless it was performed to save the mother's life or health. Any technique administered prior to implantation—for example, the therapeutic treatment given a woman immediately after rape—would be legal.

The proposed amendment was closely linked to a key point in Justice Blackmun's statement. Though the Supreme Court decreed that a state could prohibit abortion at viability, Blackmun said that the Court had to admit two facts. First, like generations of scientists, physicians, and thinkers, the Court could not definitely establish the point at which humanness begins. Second—and this is the key point—Justice Blackmun remarked that, if the fetus was actually human prior to viability, its right to life would have to be guaranteed under the Constitution.

Hence, the strategy behind the proposed amendment. Justice Blackmun had admitted that a younger fetus, if judged a human being, was entitled to the protections of the Fourteenth Amendment. So it would be necessary to adjust the Constitution to declare humanness at implantation.

Senator Buckley's measure, though the first, was certainly not the only anti-abortion proposal to take shape. The next months of 1973 saw a flood of proposed Constitutional amendments in the U.S. Senate and House of Representatives. In all, there were fifty-eight in the Senate. They were divided into two categories. In one were what Congress called "right-to-life" amendments; they were also known as "human life" amendments. The other consisted of "states rights" proposals.

There were twenty-four "right-to-life" amendments. Of that number, eighteen called for the Constitution to set humanness (or "personhood," as it was called) at a date earlier than implantation—namely, at conception—and to prohibit abortion after that point for any reason. The remaining six proposals set personhood at conception or a slightly later date, but granted exceptions for abortion. The exceptions were usually limited to the mother's health or to pregnancy resulting from rape or incest.

[53]

The "states rights" proposals numbered thirty-four. They attempted to get around the Supreme Court decision by calling for a Constitutional amendment that would give the states the right to set abortion laws for themselves. Abortion, then, would no longer be a federal matter.

When a Senator proposes a Constitutional amendment, it goes first to the Senate Judiciary Subcommittee on Constitutional Amendments. There, it is studied at length. Then, if the subcommittee feels it deserves further consideration, it is sent to the floor of the Senate for debate and action. In 1974, the subcommittee began to study the flood of proposals.

The study—headed by Subcommittee Chairman, Senator Birch Bayh of Indiana—lasted into 1975. To help them in their deliberations, the members listened to the opinions of a number of members of the clergy, medical experts, and representatives from public groups interested in abortion. The views expressed contrasted sharply, all the way from the three Catholic cardinals who called the 1973 decision "the worst mistake in the Court's history" to the arguments of those who insisted that a decision to abort was solely up to the woman.

At the end of its study, Chairman Bayh reported that the subcommittee was unable to "report out" any of the proposals. What this meant was that the subcommittee could not recommend any of the proposed amendments for the trip to the Senate floor. (The same thing happened later in the House of Representatives when a number of proposed amendments were studied by a subcommittee there.)

In explaining his subcommittee's position, Senator Bayh said that he was personally opposed to abortion. But, recognizing that so many of the views expressed to the subcommittee had been matters of personal opinion, he said that "we cannot and must not use the Constitution as an instrument for moral preference." He pointed out that the question of abortion was an "intimate one" and that the public was "deeply divided" over it, both "morally and religiously."

Senator Bayh also recognized the Constitution's separation of church and state. He said that the "private choice" of a woman to abort—as established by the Supreme Court decision—was the "Constitution's way of reconciling the irreconcilable without dangerously embroiling church and state in one another's affairs."

The subcommittee's decision not to send any of the proposed amendments to the Senate marked a serious setback for the anti-abortion forces. But it did not put an end to the controversy. By now, millions of people on both sides of the issue had organized into dedicated groups. The anti-abortionists—the "right-to-lifers," as they were now being called by the press—were determined to go on trying to alter the Court's decision. The pro-abortionists were equally determined to stop them.

THE FORCES IN
OPPOSITION

Senator Bayh couldn't have been more correct in saying that the American people were "deeply divided" over the abortion issue. That division could be clearly seen in the organizations that were now squaring off against each other.

The main organization on the anti-abortion side was the National Right to Life Committee (NRLC). Formed to lobby in Congress and in the states for a strict abortion law, the NRLC was estimated to have some 13 million members. It stated that it would support only a strong right-to-life amendment. Many anti-choice supporters, however, felt that abortion should be made legal in certain instances, particularly when the mother's health was involved.

The NRLC was supported in its stand by a number of state, local, and private groups. Among them were such diverse groups as the Minnesota Concerned Citizens for Life, and the Duke (University) Students for Life.

On the opposite—the pro-choice—side were a number of groups said to have a combined membership of around 10 million. Chief among them were the National

Abortion Rights Action League (NARAL), the Religious Coalition for Abortion Rights (RCAR), the American Civil Liberties Union (ACLU), the National Organization for Women (NOW), and the National Council of Negro Women (NCNW). Of these leading groups, only the NARAL and the RCAR were devoted exclusively to the abortion battle. Other groups, though supporting the pro-abortion movement, were also involved in other matters. NOW, for instance, was and continues to be active on all fronts working for women's rights. The ACLU is interested in all aspects of human rights and freedoms.

The pro-choice forces were also supported by a variety of religious, health and medical, legal, and civil-liberties groups. Many of them had worked earlier in activities meant to liberalize the nation's abortion laws. Every shade of opinion, from total legalization to legalization for specific reasons, was represented by the pro forces.

All the organizations, both pro and anti, took their messages to the people in meetings, radio and television interviews, and demonstrations. Anti-abortion forces still march in Washington, D.C. on every January 22—the anniversary of the 1973 decision—and send each Congressman a rose; the event, which attracted 60,000 participants in 1981, is called the "March for Life," and the rose symbolizes the lives that could be saved by a strict law. For their part, the pro-choice supporters marched in various cities, with many of the marchers carrying coat hangers and holding them aloft. The coat hanger was their symbol, the symbol of the agonies suffered by the many women who aborted themselves.

Both sides attempted to elect political candidates sympathetic to their views and to defeat those who opposed them. The anti-abortion forces were instrumental in defeating Senator Birch Bayh when he ran for reelection in 1980. Though he personally opposed abortion, they were angry with his "private choice" stand in the subcommittee hearings.

In the next year, the anti-abortion forces enjoyed another kind of victory. Legislators in Utah, feeling that the family should have some rights in abortion matters, had recently enacted a law requiring doctors in the state to inform parents when an unmarried minor sought an abortion. Behind the law was also the concern that the ease of obtaining abortions might be leading to teenage promiscuity. Pro-abortionists charged that the "free choice" intent of the 1973 decision was being undermined and tried to have the law overturned in the Supreme Court. But in 1981, the Justices ruled that, indeed, a state may require a physician to give parental notice. They went on to say, however, that the ruling did not apply to "emancipated" and "mature" minors—young people who either earn their own living or are capable of making responsible decisions for themselves. The court's ruling, however, is being disputed in several states.

Since then, Massachusetts has passed a law requiring unmarried minors to gain the consent of their parents or the courts before undergoing an abortion.

Many pro-choice supporters feel that steps such as these are opening the way to broader limitations on the availability of abortions.

MORE ACTION
IN CONGRESS

Congressional legislators, especially those opposing abortion, were as busy as the various pro- and anti-organizations in the wake of the subcommittee's refusal to "report out" any of the proposed Constitutional amendments.

For instance, Senator Jesse Helms of North Carolina, working with Senator James L. Buckley, succeeded in maneuvering an amendment past the subcommittee, using an obscure parliamentary rule to do so. The result was that, in 1976, they placed a strict "right to life" amendment on the Senate's calendar for debate and action. The bill, which was authored by Senator Helms, called for humanness—personhood—to be set at conception. The Senate debated the measure and then, despite heavy pressure from both pro- and anti-forces, tabled it for consideration at some time in the future. Plainly, with the public divided as it was, the senators found the measure too hot to handle at that time. The amendment, which made Senator Helms one of the country's best-known adversaries of abortion, remains tabled to this day and thus still available for Senate action.

In late 1981, another Constitutional amendment was proposed. Authored by Republican Senator Orrin Hatch of Utah, it calls for the following sentences to be added to the Constitution: "A right to abortion is not secured by this Constitution. The Congress and the several states shall have the concurrent power to restrict and prohibit abortion; provided that a law of the state, which is more restrictive than a law of Congress, shall prevail."

If passed, the amendment would overturn the Supreme Court's 1973 decision simply by saying that the Constitution does not grant the right to abortion. The amendment's second sentence, in addition to giving Congress and the state legislatures the right to pass restrictive and prohibitive abortion laws, would also ensure a very strict abortion law. According to the wording, a state could pass a less restrictive abortion law than Congress, but it would be overridden by a tougher Congressional act. The result: no state could have a less restrictive law than one passed by Congress.

But let's return to Senator Helms. Soon after drafting his proposed amendment, he joined forces with another legislator in a new move to negate the Supreme Court decision. That legislator was Representative Henry Hyde of Illinois. A solid foe of abortion, he had been fighting the 1973 decision in a clever and unusual way. He had attacked it by working to cut down on the amount of federal funds being made available for abortions.

For a number of years, not only Congress but also many of the states had provided monies for abortion, monies that were intended in great part to help those women who could not afford to pay for their own abortions. Representative Hyde began his attack on the federal funds in

1976 when he realized that an anti-abortion amendment might be forever in coming. The logic behind this is simple. A cut in funds might drastically reduce the abortion rate because many women, on learning that their abortions would not be financed for them, might decide to bear their children or take greater care not to become pregnant. Also, once the federal funds disappeared, the states would be left with the job of financing. Abortion would then become more an individual state matter than a federal one.

Representative Hyde was successful in his campaign. In 1976, he managed to attach an amendment to Congressional appropriation bills that limited the use of federal funds to abortions meant to safeguard the mother's health or to terminate pregnancies resulting from rape or incest. Starting in 1976, the funds were steadily reduced until, in 1981, *Time* magazine was able to report that federal support of abortions had all but ended. Some 295,000 abortions were federally funded in 1976. The number was down to just under 4,000 in 1979. It rose to just over 37,000 in 1980. The sharp decline in the number of abortions between 1976 and 1979 was in great part due to the regulations surrounding the reduced funding. Many women did not understand the regulations and so did not apply for abortion funds. Abortions rose to 37,000 in 1980 because more and more women had come to understand the regulations and the ways to go about seeking the funds.

Representative Hyde's strategy infuriated the pro-choice forces. In 1980, they took his funding restrictions to the Supreme Court and asked that they be declared unconstitutional. The Court, however, ruled that the states may refuse to pay for abortions even when medically advisable. Thus, it was constitutional to limit the funds to health, rape, and incest cases. As in the ruling pertaining to parental concern, the Court seemed to have weakened the broad intent of its 1973 decision.

A year later, in 1981, anti-abortion legislators won yet another victory. They succeeded in passing legislation that removed rape and incest cases from funding. Today, federal abortion funds are available only for women whose lives are endangered by their pregnancies.

The 1981 victory was applauded by President Ronald Reagan's administration. Commenting on it during a press conference in early 1981, Mr. Reagan said that, while dealing with California's abortion laws when governor there, he had seen that many women were fraudulently using rape or incest as an excuse to qualify for state funds.

As he made clear in his 1980 campaign for the White House, President Reagan has long been a foe of abortion. He favors national legislation that will constitutionally protect all unborn children by setting humanness at conception. On several occasions he has said that too many people, though not knowing when humanness actually begins, have chosen to think of fetuses as not yet "alive." He has then added, "I think that everything in our society calls for opting that they might be alive."

The pro-choice forces, however, see all the cuts as being grossly unfair to every woman pregnant from rape or incest, and to every pregnant woman living in a poor neighborhood. Speaking of the nation's poor, the pro-supporters point to the fact that the average cost of an abortion is $200, a sum they contend is beyond the reach of millions of desperate women who then may have to bear an unwanted child, turn to illegal but probably cheaper surgery, or be forced to abort themselves.

The 1981 cut that removed rape and incest cases from funding brought an angry reaction from *The New Republic* magazine. When the Senate passed the cut in June 1981, the magazine called the action an example of "the true mean-spiritedness of the anti-abortion movement." *The New Republic* commented that the fifty-one senators who voted for the cut weren't willing to risk the anger of anti-abortionists in their home states for the sake of the few women—about 200 or so—who annually filed for abortion funds on the grounds of rape or incest.

Today, most funding for abortions comes from the states. The amounts allotted and the conditions for their allotment are varied. In some states, such as California, the funding is broad. In others, it is kept to a minimum. In still others, pro- and anti-legislators are battling over how much money, if any, should be appropriated and for what specific reasons.

THE HELMS-HYDE BILL

As mentioned earlier, Representative Hyde and Senator Helms eventually joined forces in a new move against the Supreme Court decision. The 1980s were just dawning.

With the exception of Mr. Hyde's drive against abortion funds, all anti-abortion moves in Congress had been in the form of Constitutional amendments. Both men saw a danger to their cause in the amendment campaign—namely, that the process of enacting a Constitutional amendment is a difficult one. For passage, an amendment must be approved by two-thirds of the Congress and then be ratified by thirty-eight states. All this takes time, time in which legal abortion could become more and more a U.S. tradition and thus much harder to unseat. Further, the risk of not getting the necessary Congressional and state approvals was always great.

And so the two men opted for a simpler tactic. They introduced into Congress a bill entitled "The Human Life Statute." As a bill and not a Constitutional amendment, it would require only a simple majority vote for passage.

The Helms-Hyde bill is brief and to the point. It states: "For the purpose of enforcing the obligation of the States under the Fourteenth Amendment not to deprive persons of life without due process of law, human life shall be deemed to exist from conception." The bill then forbids abortion for any reason except to save the mother's life.

Congressional subcommittee hearings on The Human Rights Statute were held in early 1982. To date, no action has been taken on it. This is due, in great part, to the fact that Congress continues to recognize the deep public division over abortion and wants as much time as possible to think its way through to an acceptable decision; many people suspect that some legislators, not wanting to anger their pro- and anti-constituents, are avoiding a decision one way or another for as long as possible. Also, Congress is faced with many other matters, among them problems of the economy, that to most members of Congress seem to require more immediate attention.

But the bill has again triggered the old question of when human life begins. Speaking in support of the bill, anti-abortionists claim that there is present-day scientific evidence to support humanness at conception. They point to the number of scientists who argued in this direction during the subcommittee hearings.

Pro-choice supporters, however, contend that the evidence given was suspect because the testifying scientists themselves were anti-abortionists and thus gave biased testimonies.

Among those opposing the Helms-Hyde bill are some 1,300 scientists and researchers from the Massachusetts Institute of Technology and Harvard, Brandeis, and Tufts universities. In mid-1981, they signed a petition stating that "science cannot define the moment at which 'actual human life' begins" and criticizing the effort in Congress to undermine what they see as the reproductive rights of women as guaranteed by the Constitution. (Actually, some Congressional interest in the bill has waned over the past months. As a result, Senator Helms developed a companion bill in 1982. It seeks to outlaw abortion by including the fetus in the Fourteenth Amendment definition of a person. This measure—plus the Human Rights Statute and the proposed Constitutional amendments—are due for Congressional consideration some time late in 1982.)

A CONCERN ABOUT
BIRTH CONTROL MEASURES

The pro-choice forces fear the Human Rights Statute not just because it threatens the Supreme Court's 1973 decision. They see it also as opening the way to an attack on the use of contraceptive devices. In testimony during the sub-committee hearings, one scientist commented that the bill would render illegal a number of birth control measures, among them intrauterine devices (which prevent the fertilized egg from implanting itself in the uterus) and certain types of birth control pills.

Contraceptive measures are used to prevent a child from being conceived. Like abortion, contraception has long been a controversial topic throughout the world, with some moral opinion holding that it is as wrong to prevent a human life from taking shape as it is to destroy a fetus after it has developed in the mother's womb. Contrary views hold that birth control measures are necessary to keep families from becoming so large that the children are a financial and emotional burden for the parents, or for the community if the parents are not able to support them. Accompanying this view is the feeling that there must be definite control exercised over family size if the world is not to become over-populated.

The contraception debate is not often heard today. At one time, however, it raged quite as fiercely as the current abortion controversy.

When, in the late 1800s, the use of contraceptive measures was first advocated in England and on the continent of Europe, it was greeted with protest and rage by many people. The same thing happened here in the United States in the early twentieth century when doctors began giving their patients birth control advice. The physicians were not only severely criticized in many quarters but were also threatened with arrest.

An early champion of birth control in America, Margaret Sanger, came to the defense of the doctors in one of her magazines. She argued that doctors had a right to give such advice and that parents had the right to regulate the size of their families. She said that the need for birth control had been impressed upon her when she had worked as a nurse among poor families in New York City. She had seen a tragically high death rate among the newborn infants of these families and had seen much economic misery and poor health among families that had grown too large.

Mrs. Sanger was both praised and criticized for her views. She did not, however, limit her support of birth control to her magazines. She founded the American Birth Control League in the early 1920s and then helped to organize the Birth Control Clinical Research Bureau. These two organizations merged in 1939 to become the Birth Control Federation of America. In 1942, the name of the organization was changed to the one now familiar to the whole country—the Planned Parenthood Federation of America.

Because of the efforts of such pioneers as Margaret Sanger, birth control is a widely accepted practice in the United States today. In general, Americans feel that the use of birth control measures is a matter of personal choice and conscience.

But now the pro-choice supporters in the abortion debate are fearful that, should the Helms-Hyde statute be enacted, the more zealous of their opponents will use it as grounds for attempting to outlaw contraceptives. The result: another area of private decision will be threatened with government regulation. The abortion controversy will be joined by a complex issue that everyone considered settled years ago.

THE CONTROVERSY TODAY

Today, the abortion controversy leaves Americans with five possible legal options. Do the majority want the Constitutional amendments proposed by Senators Helms and Hatch, or the Helms-Hyde statute? Or the new Helms bill, which includes the fetus in the Fourteenth Amendment's definition of a person? Or do they favor a more stringent law, one that outlaws abortion from conception on, for any reason? Or are they happy with the Supreme Court's 1973 decision? Or would they favor some law that would fall somewhere between these extremes, perhaps one that allows abortions until a later date in pregnancy but specifies that they can be performed only for certain reasons?

The controversy seems to be divided along political party lines. If you look at a list of the most ardent anti-abortion legislators, you'll find that virtually all are conservative Republicans. They are supported by the most conservative elements of the general public, including the Moral Majority, which has become a strong nationwide force in recent years. Pro-abortion is heavily represented by Democratic legislators, by some of the more liberal Republicans, and by liberal-minded segments of the population.

The division alarms pro-choice advocates because the early 1980s have witnessed a strong political and social trend toward conservatism in the United States. It's a trend that can most plainly be seen in the election of Ronald Reagan as president. Pro-abortionists are fearful that, with a strong anti-abortion supporter in the White House, the chances are great that Congress will enact a strict abortion measure sometime during the decade.

And there is no doubt that Mr. Reagan is a strong supporter of the anti-abortion movement. At his early 1982 press conference, he voiced again his often-repeated view that, even if we do not know whether a fetus is human at conception, we should give it the benefit of doubt and "opt for life." He backed this opinion with the example of the drowning man who, on being pulled from the water, gives "every appearance of being dead." But instead of depending on appearances, we assume that he's still alive and make every attempt to revive him until we are certain that our efforts are in vain. The same consideration should be given the fetus, Reagan said.

But anti-abortionists have reason to be concerned, too, as they look forward into the 1980s. Surveys have recently been made to assess public opinion on abortion. In general, they reveal a liberal outlook on the issue. For instance, a

Gallup poll taken in 1980 showed that those polled opposed a ban on all abortions by a wide margin—67 percent opposed, 33 percent favored a ban.

There were similar findings in a CBS–*New York Times* poll in 1981. Of the people questioned, 68 percent felt that a woman should be allowed to have an abortion if she wanted one and if her doctor agreed. Only 25 percent thought that she should be barred from having the operation. The remaining people polled were undecided on the question.

A recent ABC–Harris poll revealed that 60 percent of the people questioned approved of the Supreme Court's 1973 decision. The decision was opposed by 37 percent of those polled.

And recent surveys by the National Research Center show that between 82 and 91 percent of the people questioned approved of abortion in cases involving rape, incest, and the mother's health. At the same time, however, only between 47 and 52 percent favored abortion for other, less compelling, reasons.

And so, in light of the conservative political trend in the nation as opposed to what public opinion seems to be, thoughtful Americans can only wonder what the outcome of the abortion controversy will be. Perhaps the coming years of the 1980s will tell us.

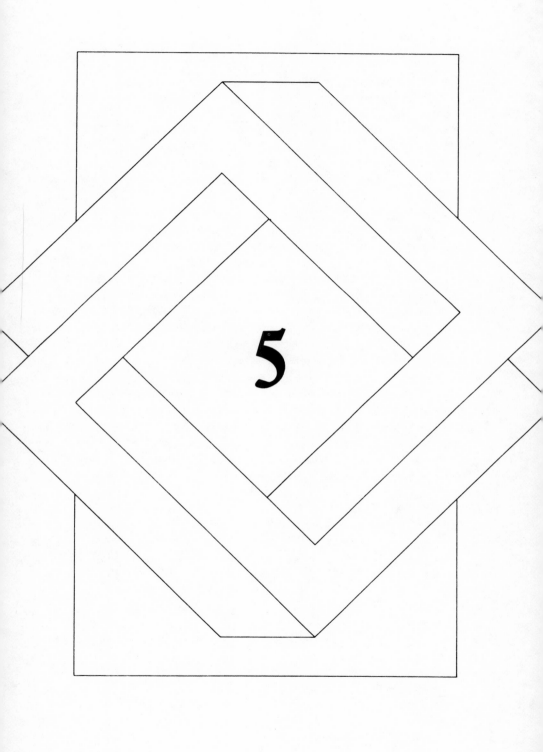

THE EUTHANASIA CONTROVERSY

With this chapter, we come to the second of the great "matters of life and death" facing people during the 1980s—euthanasia. It provokes a question that, though involving a similar moral dilemma, is exactly opposite to that posed by abortion. Abortion causes us to wonder if we have the right to end a life before birth. Now we must ask if we have the right to end life *after* birth with the practice of euthanasia.

The term *euthanasia* comes from ancient Greece and is a combination of the Greek words meaning *good* (or *easy*) and *death*. It is defined as the act of ending a life in as gentle and painless a way as possible. Specifically, it refers to ending a life to prevent further suffering and pain when a person is enduring a hopeless illness that, ultimately, will bring only death.

Under the definition, the life may be ended by another person or by the sufferer himself or herself. Suicide, then, is seen as a form of euthanasia.

[69]

Because it refers to death being brought on for reasons of compassion and pity, euthanasia has long been called "mercy killing." This term was once widely used by people everywhere, but is now considered too sensational. It's to be found only in the press and never in medical practice.

ACTIVE AND
PASSIVE EUTHANASIA

Modern medical science is able to keep a patient alive long past the time when, in earlier days, he or she would surely have died. This has caused euthanasia to be divided into two types—active and passive.

Active euthanasia is the act of deliberately killing an incurably ill patient. For example, no longer able to stand the thought of someone suffering so much, the doctor, a friend, or a relative ends the patient's life with poison. Or perhaps the patient is given a medicinal drug in such a quantity that death will shortly follow.

Passive euthanasia is possible because medicine now has many aids for prolonging a patient's life. They include medications, treatments, and mechanical life support systems such as respirators that help a patient to continue breathing. Passive euthanasia means that these aids are withdrawn or withheld from an incurably ill patient if further care promises no chance of bringing about some sort of recovery.

In the knowledge that death is certain, that the illness is bringing great suffering, and that the life-sustaining measures can do no real good, the patient is made as comfortable as possible and is allowed to die.

Active euthanasia is looked on as a moral wrong—and thus a crime—in most parts of the world. It is generally conceded to be the equivalent of murder or, at the least, because it is prompted by mercy—manslaughter. Consequently, there is little controversy to be heard about the rightness or wrongness of active euthanasia.

It is passive euthanasia that is at the heart of today's

controversy. Like abortion, it has divided the world's people into camps of opposing viewpoints. On one side are those who support the idea of passive euthanasia because they feel it is cruel to keep a patient alive and suffering when death is all that the future holds. Many of their number also argue that it must be against God's will to keep a person alive by artificial means when he or she would have died a natural death without such support.

Contrasting sharply with these viewpoints are the people opposed to passive euthanasia under any circumstances. Many of their number feel that life is so precious that every possible effort should be made to see that it is sustained. And many see life as the Creator's work and argue that God alone holds the privilege of taking it away.

As in the abortion controversy, there is a "middle ground" camp. It is made up of people who think that passive euthanasia should neither be completely outlawed nor completely allowed. Rather, they feel that the decision to withdraw or withhold life-sustaining treatment should be made on a case-by-case basis. The decision would depend on what the doctor and the family thought to be the wisest and most humane course, and on what the patient wished.

These are the most basic positions in the controversy. Other beliefs are also being voiced on all sides. We'll talk of them shortly.

Because most of the advanced medical techniques for sustaining life have been developed in recent times, passive euthanasia is a relatively new concept. But there is nothing new about euthanasia itself. It is a practice as old as abortion.

EUTHANASIA
IN HISTORY

Euthanasia dates far back in the history of all parts of the world. From the most ancient times, both young and old people were subjected to euthanasia.

Despite the fact that it is mainly used for reasons of mercy, the earliest recorded instances of euthanasia seem to have had little to do with kindness. Rather, they are examples of societies controlling their populations by disposing of the people whom they did not see as useful.

A case in point is the ancient Greek city of Sparta, which was famous for its citizens' military prowess. Strong young men who would make fine soldiers were greatly admired. It was common practice in Sparta to kill children who were weak or sick and thus, as the early historian, Plutarch, wrote, "ill-suited from birth for health and vigor." Mercy may have played a part in the killing of those children who were suffering acute pain because of illness. But, in the main, Sparta wanted only a certain type of citizen.

However, most victims of euthanasia were old people who were so ill or enfeebled that they could contribute little or nothing to their society. At the same time, they were consumers of an always meager food supply. In India, it was once customary to throw old people into the Ganges River and allow them to drown. On the Mediterranean island of Sardinia, ancient custom called for sons to club their aged fathers to death.

In a number of societies, tradition demanded that the old commit voluntary euthanasia—namely, take their own lives or, as was probably the case in Sardinia and India, submit themselves willingly to death by other hands. Possibly the most famous example of voluntary euthanasia comes to us from the Eskimos. Their aged went out on the ice, or allowed themselves to be carried there, so that they could freeze to death.

Many of the world's early thinkers were in favor of euthanasia. Pythagoras of Greece and Cicero of Rome, for instance, commented that voluntary euthanasia was morally correct, an unselfish act by people who realized that they were no longer useful contributors to their society. In Greece, Aristotle condoned the Spartan practice of killing physically and mentally weak children, and Plato argued that suicide was a legitimate way for a person to put an end to unendurable pain.

Early on, however, people began to regard euthanasia as a moral wrong and the death practices of some societies as cruel. The major religions—Judaism, Christianity, and Islam—were greatly responsible for this change of attitude.

All the religions regarded life as sacred, the work of the Creator. If life lasted beyond the point of usefulness, if it advanced into crippling infirmity or heartbreaking senility, or if it ended in excruciating pain, then that was the will of the Creator and somehow a part of His grand design for humanity. No one must interfere. Both euthanasia and suicide were branded as great moral wrongs.

In Judaism, for instance, the term for euthanasia— *mitah yafah* (pleasant death)—always referred to the giving of comfort to criminals facing execution and not to the act of ending the life of someone already dying from natural causes. Seeing life as being of inestimable value, the Jewish people saw each facet of life as important. Thus, in the Jewish faith, a patient on his or her deathbed is considered as a living person in every respect. Nothing may be done to cause that person to die quickly, though measures can be taken to alleviate pain. Any killing of an innocent person, regardless of whether healthy or about to die from natural causes, was seen by the Jewish people as murder.

This view continues in modern times, though there is a segment of Jewish opinion today that sees passive euthanasia as morally acceptable. We'll talk more about this later.

In the Christian era, a number of great philosophers opposed euthanasia. Among them were St. Thomas Aquinas and St. Augustine. In the thirteenth century, Thomas Aquinas wrote that when a man took his own or another's life, he was usurping God's power over life and death. Earlier, in the sixth century, Augustine pointed out that nowhere in the Scriptures does it say that man was authorized to take an innocent human life; man, therefore, had no grounds for assuming such authority. St. Augustine's logic serves as the base for the Catholic Church's opposition to euthanasia.

It must be said immediately, however, that the Catholic view of euthanasia has long been influenced by what is known as the "double effect" principle. Developed centuries ago by Catholic thinkers, it is similar to the direct-versus-indirect-killing concept in abortion. The principle holds that an action that is primarily intended to relieve pain and suffering may be ethically correct even though it involves the secondary effect of possibly causing death. As we'll see later, this principle underlies today's body of Catholic opinion that finds passive euthanasia acceptable in a variety of circumstances.

The view of active euthanasia as a moral wrong has prevailed worldwide through the centuries. There have always been, however, opposing outlooks expressed by thinkers who contended that the deliberate taking of a life in pain was both humane and moral. Among such thinkers were two internationally renowned philosophers of the eighteenth century—David Hume in Great Britain and Immanuel Kant in Germany.

And history has been punctuated by instances of societies acting contrary to the world view. The greatest example of state-sponsored euthanasia in our century was seen in Nazi Germany. Under Adolf Hitler in the 1930s, the nation set up a number of euthanasia clinics. A board of government officials and physicians was assigned the task of dispatching to the clinics anyone who was suffering an incurable illness or who, for various reasons, was judged no longer fit to lead a useful and productive life. In practice, many people were condemned to the clinics because of political or religious opposition to the Nazi regime.

The concentration camps that were established under Hitler to rid Europe of its Jewish population were seen as centers for euthanasia as well as genocide. (Genocide means the deliberate and systematic destruction of a racial, political, or cultural group.) This is because the prisoners chosen for extermination in the camp gas chambers were usually picked on the basis of age and poor health. The strong were allowed to stay alive for a while longer so that they could work as slave laborers for the state.

EUTHANASIA
AND THE LAW

Because it was viewed as murder and as an interference with God's power over life and death, the early laws governing euthanasia were as strict as those for abortion. Sentences could range from long imprisonment to death. Later, though the laws remained strict, a number of societies seemed hesitant to apply harsh penalties. This was especially true in societies where the jury system was used. Many jurors were reluctant to punish offenders whose crimes had been motivated by compassion and pity.

Then, as happened with abortion, our century saw a move first in Europe and then the United States to liberalize the laws. The change stemmed from two new and growing outlooks—first, that the incurably ill might after all have the right to ask that their lives be mercifully ended and, second, that it did not seem right to place a mercy killer, prompted as he or she might have been by the most sympathetic of motives, in the same class with other murderers.

As a result, a number of nations now call for the authorities to take into account the motivation behind a mercy killing. By looking at the motives, the authorities seek to establish the severity of the offense. In this way, a person who kills out of a real sense of pity will not be regarded in the same manner as a killer who, say, takes the life of a terminally ill relative under the guise of compassion when the actual motive is to acquire the victim's wealth.

Among the countries using such an approach are

[75]

Poland and the Soviet Union; there, the penalty for mercy killing is adjusted in cases where deep pity is evident and in cases where the victim is known to have asked for death. In Switzerland and West Germany, a mercy killer is not charged with homicide but with a lesser crime.

Norway treats euthanasia not as murder but as a special kind of crime requiring special handling. The type of punishment is decided by the trial judge. This method prevents a jury opposed to euthanasia from giving the defendant too harsh a penalty, and a pro-euthanasia jury from treating him or her too lightly. The judges in such cases may personally be for or against euthanasia; however, because of their sense of professional responsibility and their devotion to the law, it is presumed that, more than might be possible for a jury, they will be guided by the legal facts involved and not by emotion. A problem with jury trials has long been the danger that a wrong verdict will be rendered on the basis of emotion.

Though euthanasia laws have been made less strict over the past years, only one country in the world has gone so far as to legalize euthanasia completely. In 1933, the Latin American nation, Uruguay, decreed in its Penal Code that a mercy killer would be totally safe from criminal prosecution.

Historically, in the United States, the development of euthanasia laws has been left to the states. In general, U.S. laws hold that a person who kills for reasons of mercy, or assists a sufferer to commit suicide, is a murderer. People who kill themselves or ask to be killed are, also technically at least, guilty of a crime—suicide.

A mercy killer can be charged with various degrees of homicide. Manslaughter is usually the least of the possible counts. A sentence for manslaughter can range from several years to life in prison.

Though U.S. laws are strict, the treatment shown a mercy killer has often been lenient. This has been principally due to sympathetic judges and juries.

Up to now in the historical sections of this chapter, we've been talking about active euthanasia. Now we must begin discussing passive euthanasia. This new concept is causing Americans to take another look at the country's euthanasia laws.

EUTHANASIA
AND MEDICINE

Any discussion of passive euthanasia must begin with the physician. Living in an age when life-sustaining procedures have come into increasing use, the doctor has had to face a bewildering problem.

The problem centers about the oath that all physicians take at the outset of their careers. Known as the Hippocratic oath, it comes from the ancient Greek medical figure, Hippocrates (fourth century B.C.), and calls on physicians to dedicate their lives to preserving life and relieving pain. Further, they swear that to no patient "will I give a deadly drug even if solicited, nor offer counsel to such an end."

Doctors take the oath seriously. But, as life-sustaining procedures were developed over the years, many physicians realized that they were being put into an impossible situation.

On the one hand they could see that, when they prolonged a life that was in the last and most painful stages of an incurable illness, they seemed to be betraying their promise to relieve the patient's suffering. But on the other hand, if they didn't do everything possible to sustain the patient's life, they seemed to be violating their pledge to preserve life.

Each physician handled the problem in his or her own way. Some opted to provide all the life-sustaining treatment necessary; many believed that this was the moral and professionally ethical step to take. Many others felt that by doing so they were acting incorrectly but that, in the light of their Hippocratic oath and the laws against euthanasia, there was no other choice open to them. Some elected to withdraw the treatment quietly at the request of the patient or family. Others, while employing the life-sustaining measures, provided them in as little degree as possible so that the patient would not suffer too long.

Still others found ways to shift the problem to the patient's family. One strategy was often used when a patient was being cared for at home. The physician would give the drugs that were needed for the patient's care to the family. He or she would inform the family of the correct dosage and then mention the lethal consequences should an overdose be administered. The physician did not advise that an overdose be given. The family was simply told of the consequences, and any decision concerning what to do with the drugs was left to them. Technically at least, the provisions of the Hippocratic oath had been met. The physician had neither administered a "deadly drug" nor counseled that it be used.

But none of these approaches were satisfactory. None solved the problem. Some new solution had to be found that would balance compassion for the patient with the demands of the Hippocratic oath and the moral prohibition against murder.

A possible solution sprang to mind—the concept of passive euthanasia. It was based on the inescapable fact that every human being must inevitably die, and it was intended for use in only those cases in which life-sustaining measures had no chance of bringing about a recovery. In such instances, would it not be moral and professionally ethical to withhold or withdraw such measures in the final stages of an incurable illness and let nature, as it has always done, claim the patient? Much unnecessary pain would be avoided. Physicians would be honoring their oath neither to cause suffering nor to administer a "deadly" treatment. They would simply be stepping aside and bowing to the demands of nature.

The concept struck many doctors and much of the public as just and reasonable. They could see that patients in the last stages of illnesses such as cancer were suffering great pain. They could see that many of the life-sustaining measures—shots that had to be given on a regular basis, various tests that had to be made to determine a patient's exact condition, and tubes that had to be inserted into the nose to assist breathing—were uncomfortable for the patient and at times painful.

But just as many other people found the "passive" concept objectionable. As was said earlier, they deeply believed that life is so precious that no one should do anything to end it—only God, not man, had the right to take a life. The result: today's controversy over passive euthanasia took shape and began to spread throughout the United States as well as all countries where the concept was under discussion.

Right from the start, there was the problem of whether passive euthanasia would be accepted in the eyes of the law. After all, it was still euthanasia, and euthanasia was strictly forbidden. The laws were all specifically directed at active euthanasia, of course, but some were so worded that they could be interpreted as also forbidding passive euthanasia.

One such interpretation came from the assistant attorney general of the state of Washington. In 1977, he said that, under the present law of his state, "an attempt to bring about death by the removal of a life-sustaining mechanism would constitute homicide, first degree."

And so the question loomed: was it murder to allow a person to die by failing to use some method that would uselessly preserve life? The nation got its first answer to that question in the 1970s.

KAREN ANN QUINLAN

In the summer of 1975, twenty-one-year-old Karen Ann Quinlan lay dying in a New Jersey hospital. While attending a party several months earlier, she had suddenly become ill and fallen into a coma from which she had never awakened. The cause of her illness was unknown. But after extensive tests and various treatments, the doctors agreed that she had suffered irreversible brain damage and was doomed; even if by some miracle she managed to survive, she would have to be institutionalized for the rest of her life. She was being kept alive by a respirator that was connected to her trachea, and maintained her breathing.

Her watching parents endured a double tragedy. They felt that Karen was hopelessly ill. And they felt that she was suffering great pain; in her coma, her body was contorted, her head was constantly moving, and she was moaning. Heartbroken, they asked that the respirator be removed so that their daughter could die in peace. The request was refused. Though many of the people involved in the case felt deep sympathy for the Quinlans, both the hospital and the medical personnel had been advised by lawyers that, if the respirator was discontinued and if Karen then died, they might be open to prosecution on criminal charges or malpractice. There was also the deep feeling among many of the medical personnel that their job was to preserve life at all costs, not take it.

The Quinlans went to court in an effort to have the respirator removed. They faced opposing arguments that not only was euthanasia illegal but that removal would be unfair to Karen becaue she was not conscious and able to say for herself whether she wished to live or die. But the parents eventually won their case. In 1976 the New Jersey Supreme Court ruled it legal for doctors to discontinue the operation of a mechanical device that is keeping a doomed and comatose patient uselessly alive. In its ruling, the court called for a medical committee to be formed to help the doctors determine in which future cases the use of the mechanical device should be discontinued. (At the time this book is being written, Karen Quinlan remains alive.)

Behind the decision there seemed to be the belief that the use of extraordinary means to sustain life in the final stages of a terminal illness can constitute an indignity to the patient. Several magazines, when commenting on the case, stated that such means can take the patient's human dignity away. The attempt to keep the body alive—and not the patient himself or herself—seems to become the important thing. This is an injustice to the patient.

The Court also recognized, as many physicians were recognizing, that the use of extraordinary means accomplished little other than prolonged suffering for the patient and the grieving family. These expensive means, too, could ruin a family financially.

The decision was an historic one. It was the beginning of a legal basis for the use of passive euthanasia. And, as the U.S. Supreme Court's 1973 decision had done in the area of abortion, it caused the controversy to spread further.

Much has happened since the Quinlan case as the various states have sought to settle the legality of passive euthanasia. In the next chapter, we'll see all that has been happening. But we need to open the chapter with a close look at the opposing sides in the controversy so that we can see exactly what they stand for.

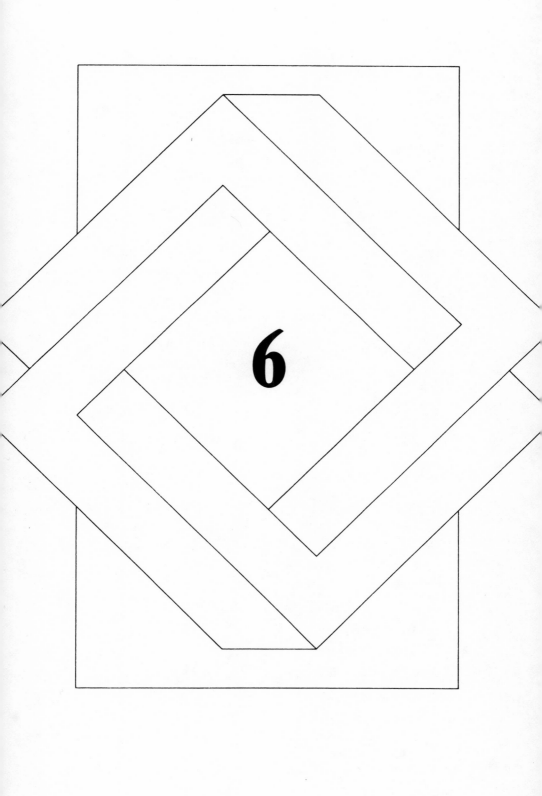

FOR AND AGAINST
EUTHANASIA

Let's begin our look at the two sides in the controversy by turning to the opinions of the many people who are opposed to passive euthanasia.

AGAINST EUTHANASIA

The press now refers to opponents of euthanasia as vitalists; the term stems from the word *vital*, which has a variety of definitions, one of them being "characteristic of life or living beings." The vitalists earned their name because of their deep belief that life is so precious that it must never be ended other than by natural causes. The religious of their number see life as being the Creator's handiwork and thus should be free from human intervention.

To all vitalists, euthanasia of any kind, whether it be active or passive, is an act that devalues the sanctity of life. In addition to these basic beliefs, vitalists oppose passive euthanasia on several counts.

For one, they fear that many a patient could be condemned to death on being judged terminal when, in fact, he or she might not be beyond recovery. They substantiate this fear by pointing to the rapid advances in treatment procedures and equipment that are the hallmark of modern medicine. Such advances make it highly possible for many of today's incurable patients to become tomorrow's curable patients. All patients, then, should be afforded every opportunity to survive until that tomorrow arrives.

There is also always the chance, vitalists argue, of a mistaken diagnosis by the doctors; rather than turning to euthanasia, doctors should seek to ease a patient's suffering by examining the illness more closely and attempting other treatments that might lead to a cure. And there is always the chance that an incurable illness such as cancer will go into remission—that is, mysteriously halt its advance for an undetermined amount of time, perhaps for months or years. If passive euthanasia is practiced, many patients might well die just before their illness is about to go into remission. Years of precious life could be lost.

A story of remission is told by Dr. Christiaan Barnard, the talented and highly respected South African physician who pioneered heart transplant surgery in the 1960s. It must be noted immediately that Dr. Barnard has said he favors passive euthanasia. He believes that even active euthanasia might have a place in medicine, but does not practice it himself. In an interview for *People* magazine in 1981, however, he spoke of how he had once been tempted to take a patient's life.

He recalled that his patient was a young woman suffering so terribly in the advanced stages of cancer that, as he put it, she begged God to take her life. Deeply moved by her anguish, one night Barnard filled a syringe with a lethal dose of morphine—twelve times the normal dosage—and went to her room. But he could not bring himself to administer the drug. He felt that he would be doing the same thing as slitting her throat. A few weeks later, he saw the young woman leave the hospital with her husband.

The patient who might have died at his hands had been undergoing radium therapy, and it had helped to bring on a period of remission.

One aspect of passive euthanasia is of particular concern to many vitalists. When the decision to withhold or withdraw life-sustaining equipment must be made, many patients have already slipped into the coma that often accompanies the final stages of an illness. And many other patients, such as the elderly, may be incapable of speaking for themselves. In cases such as these, the patients have no say in their fate. The decision for death is left to someone else—to the doctors, to the family, or to both. This, the vitalists contend, is a gross injustice to the patients. Human beings who might desperately want to live are condemned to death because they are without a voice to raise in protest.

As for those patients who are able to speak, some face moments of such intense pain that they beg for death. These pleas, vitalists argue, should not automatically be taken at face value. There may be other moments when, in less pain, a patient would want to go on surviving. But, should they fall into a coma before that time, they will be condemned to death on the basis of a momentary feeling that was not really their true wish.

The vitalists also worry that comatose or mentally incompetent patients can easily become the victims of family decisions that are made out of frustration, or even heartlessness. Perhaps the family members agree to let a patient die because the illness is placing a terrible economic burden on them. Or perhaps there are unscrupulous relatives who are eager to inherit the patient's wealth. The defenseless patient is condemned to death on the pretense of compassion when, in reality, other motives may be at work.

Finally, vitalists fear that the acceptance of passive euthanasia will cause society to regard as less valuable the sanctity of human life. As they see it, ending the lives of the incurably ill could be just a step away from justifying the deliberate elimination of all people judged to be unfit by a society. The old, the unproductive, the mentally deficient, the physically weak—all could then become the victims of active euthanasia in a society that has decided it is best to foster only the strong. And there is the danger that some ruthless leader could employ euthanasia to be rid of political, religious, or ethnic enemies. This sort of tragedy has happened before—remember Sparta in ancient Greece, and Germany in our century—and it could happen again.

FOR EUTHANASIA

The people who support passive euthanasia feel that it is pointless to burden a doomed patient with measures that will sustain life a while longer but that will do nothing to effect a recovery. Rather, it is both humane and moral to hasten death and thus relieve the patient of pain. Death must come anyway. What, then, is the purpose of trying to avoid the inevitable and subjecting the patient to an additional period of anguish in the process?

In exact opposition to the vitalist belief that euthanasia devalues life, the supporters hold that the useless prolonging of life demeans it. They argue that it is the quality of life that counts, not mere physical existence. The awful pain of a terminal illness and the discomfort that so often accompanies life-sustaining treatment are assaults on that quality and can strip the patient of human dignity. These are insults to life. In the name of compassion, we should do all we reasonably can to make doomed and suffering patients comfortable and allow them to die with their dignity intact.

The same compassion, in the eyes of euthanasia supporters, should be extended to terminal patients who ask for death or who are destined to linger on in a vegetable-like pain-wracked state.

In all the above instances—and especially in cases of lingering death—the supporters see in passive euthanasia not only compassion for the sufferer but also for the family members who must stand by and watch a loved one in pain.

Supporters of euthanasia find society's attitude toward passive euthanasia illogical and hypocritical. In his *People* magazine interview, Dr. Christiaan Barnard pointed out that humanity long ago accepted the right of nations to send millions of men to their deaths in war. He added that, in most countries today, the defense budget outstrips by far the amounts allocated for health care and welfare programs. He then commented that people also accept the right of the courts to sentence a human being to death for a capital crime. But society balks at the idea of allowing doctors to hasten death for a suffering, terminally ill patient. To Dr. Barnard, the situation makes no sense.

Many euthanasia supporters, Dr. Barnard among them, disagree with the vitalist contention that people have no right to interfere with God's handiwork. The South African doctor, again speaking in the *People* interview, remarked that physicians are intervening in God's work— "playing God" themselves—when they use life-sustaining measures that do nothing but prolong life beyond the time when death could have been expected. He said that he does not think a merciful Creator is angered when sympathetic doctors "play God" by hastening death in hopeless cases.

The supporters also disagree with the vitalist argument that passive euthanasia will too often allow a comatose patient to be condemned to death by relatives whose motives are financial rather than compassionate. There are, they contend, many factors that work against this possibility. For one, many relatives are loving and honorable and want to do only what is right and humane. For another, the decision to withhold or withdraw treatment is usually made in consultation with a physician (whose Hippocratic oath, remember, makes it difficult for him or her to consider euthanasia). All aspects of a patient's condition and future are discussed before any decision is reached. Further, laws can be developed to protect a patient against the

[89]

possible misuse of the practice. For instance, as was done in the New Jersey decision in the Karen Quinlan case, the laws can call for the formation of medical committees to help doctors decide when euthanasia is the best course. They could also allow passive euthanasia for patients who have expressed their wish to die by making out what is called a "living will." We'll talk more about living wills later.

Many supporters also argue that, while the rights of the patient must always come first, the family situation should also be given consideration. Suppose that a patient's illness is placing an economic burden on the family that is simply too much for them to bear. Is it right and just to maintain a doomed life with measures that will not alter the outcome of the illness but that, in the meantime, may well ruin a family financially and result in long years of hardship? There is a strong feeling among many supporters that the family and its needs deserve consideration and protection as well as the patient.

Those who favor passive euthanasia have received much encouragement from modern religious thought. Let's turn to where today's faiths stand in the controversy.

THE RELIGIOUS VIEW

As in the past, leaders of the world's major religions continue to regard active euthanasia as murder and thus morally wrong. But passive euthanasia is proving to be a different matter. Many Protestant, Jewish, and Catholic thinkers argue that it can be both a moral and a humane act.

At the base of their concern are the pointless suffering and the loss of human dignity that attend the use of life-sustaining measures. Religious thinkers recognize that life is to be revered and that it must be closely cared for, but that it also must, sooner or later, end. To them, the reverence for life includes allowing it to end as peacefully and as gracefully as possible, free of further pain and further assaults on one's dignity.

[90]

As you'll recall from chapter 5, Jewish teaching has always held that life and every facet of it is of infinite value and, therefore, must not be ended in any but a natural way. But many rabbis today are pointing to another teaching in the *Talmud* (the ancient book of Jewish tradition and law) as justification for passive euthanasia. This teaching permits the removal of an impediment to a person's natural death—in the words of the *Talmud*, an impediment such as "clattering noise or salt on his tongue" that delays "the departure of his soul." As some rabbis see it, a life-sustaining measure or device, if it does nothing other than keep the hopelessly ill patient alive beyond his or her time, can be branded an impediment to a natural death. As such, its removal—or the decision not to use it—would be permissible.

In their own ways, the Catholic Church and many Protestant denominations likewise see the use of life-sustaining measures as impediments to a natural and dignified death. For centuries (again as you'll recall from chapter 5), the Catholic Church has not opposed certain instances of euthanasia on the grounds of the "double effect" principle. The principle holds that an action whose primary intent is to relieve pain may be used even if it has the secondary effect of possibly causing the patient's death. Suppose that you administer a pain-killing drug that then causes the patient's death. According to the principle, you are free of moral guilt if your primary intent was to relieve suffering and not to kill the patient.

Using the "double effect" principle, the Church feels that extraordinary medical measures can be removed or withheld in the name of the patient's comfort even if this action may result in death. The withholding or the removal is seen as an indirect and not a direct cause of the death; a direct cause, which is forbidden, would be, for example, the deliberate administration of a drug in lethal dose.

The Catholic view of passive euthanasia was stated in 1957 by Pope Pius XII. In a paper titled *The Prolongation of Life*, the Pope held that a patient's family is bound to use what he called "ordinary means of care"—care that com-

[91]

forts and attempts to bring about a recovery and thus has a direct effect on the patient's survival. But, on turning to extraordinary measures, the Pope commented that their withdrawal is "never more than an indirect cause of the cessation of life." Therefore, he said, it is proper for a doctor to "remove the artificial respiration apparatus before the blood circulation has come to a complete stop."

In 1980, Pope John Paul II added to this view. When commenting on the progress of medical science in recent years, he said:

"When inevitable death is imminent in spite of the means used, it is permitted in conscience to take the decision to refuse forms of treatment that would only secure a precarious and burdensome prolongation of life, so long as the normal care due to a sick person in similar cases is not interrupted."

PASSIVE EUTHANASIA
AND THE LAW

As we saw earlier, the euthanasia controversy has been in full flower since the New Jersey Supreme Court decision in the Karen Ann Quinlan case. The opposing views in the debate are firmly held and often heatedly voiced by their advocates. In the midst of the conflicting arguments, the states and the courts have spent much of their time in recent years attempting to settle the legality of passive euthanasia.

The 1976 decision in the Quinlan case started passive euthanasia on the road to legality. But since the decision came from just one state, it was no more than that—a start. The legality of passive euthanasia remained a question mark in all the other states.

Nor did the decision settle matters for all the medical people in New Jersey itself. Many doctors and hospital personnel were outraged that they had been given legal permission to allow their patients to die through the withdrawal of life-sustaining treatment. They were dedicated to preserving life and to the Hippocratic oath. They refused to take advantage of the decision.

Soon after the Quinlan decision, euthanasia cases came to court in four other states—Delaware, Florida, Massachusetts, and New York. All were brought by the friends or relatives of patients who, comatose or incompetent, were incapable of speaking for themselves. All asked that the patients be freed of pointless life-sustaining measures.

The fact that the patients were comatose or incompetent must be remembered here. A basic legal question in passive euthanasia has always centered about such patients. It asks: are a patient's human rights violated when life-sustaining measures are removed at a time when he or she is unable to express any desires one way or the other concerning such drastic action? Conscious and alert patients are seen as being able to defend their own human rights.

The cases concluded with decisions favoring the removal of life-sustaining measures. But the courts set definite limits on the removal. For instance, the New York Court of Appeals, the highest court in that state, ruled that removal was permissible only if: (1) there was no hope of the patient recovering and (2) there was "clear and convincing" evidence that the patient, when yet conscious and competent, had stated that he or she wanted no extraordinary treatment if and when the time came for such a decision to be made.

These same two stipulations had been important in the Quinlan trial. Karen Ann's parents had won the case by establishing her condition as hopeless and by presenting evidence of her wishes. They testified that, on several occasions before falling sick, she had remarked that she would prefer death rather than painful and useless extraordinary treatment were she ever to become terminally ill.

The four euthanasia cases proved difficult for the people who brought them to court. First, the trials took time—precious time during which the patients continued to suffer. Second, the trials involved a heavy expense. Third—and perhaps most important of all—they put a terrible burden on the individual families to present evidence of the involved patient's true wishes. The evidence, as in the words of the New York Court of Appeals, had to be "clear and convincing." Hearsay evidence (evidence based not on a witness's personal knowledge but information supplied by someone else) wouldn't do. Nor would someone's opinion of what the patient might want. Nor would some vague remark once made by the patient. Precise information on the patient's desires was needed.

The problem was a major one and there seemed but one way to solve it. When still conscious and competent—perhaps in the first stages of illness or even before falling ill—a person had to express his or her wishes for the future in a statement that would be legally acceptable. Thus, the idea for what is now called "the living will" was born.

The living will is a written document in which a person clearly states that he or she does not wish to be given extraordinary treatment when helplessly caught in the final stages of illness. In the will, the person may spell out the life values that make such treatment repugnant. The document usually names one or two other persons who are authorized to see that the provisions of the will are carried out as stipulated. It is witnessed by one or more persons at the time it is signed.

Once the will is written and signed, the signer is free to change his or her mind. The will can then be revoked and the request for extraordinary treatment made.

The living will may come in many different forms, though the contents of each are substantially the same. A representative example of a living will appeared in a 1976 issue of The New England Journal of Medicine. Developed by ethics teacher Sissela Bok, it carefully stipulates the various circumstances under which extraordinary care is to be discontinued or not to be used in the first place. The will reads:

DIRECTIONS FOR MY CARE

I wish to live a full and long life, but not at all costs: If my death is near and cannot be avoided, and if I have lost the ability to interact with others and have no reasonable chance of regaining this ability, or if my suffering is intense and irreversible, I do not want to have my life prolonged. I would then ask not to be subjected to surgery or resuscitation. Nor would I then wish to have life support from mechanical ventilators, intensive care services, or other life prolonging procedures, including the administration of antibiotics and blood products. I would wish, rather, to have care which gives comfort and support, which facilitates my interaction with others to the extent that this is possible, and which brings peace.

In order to carry out these instructions and to interpret them, I authorize_____to accept, plan, and refuse treatment on my behalf in cooperation with attending physicians and health personnel. This person knows how I value the experience of living, and how I would weigh incompetence, suffering, and dying. Should it be impossible to reach this person, I authorize _____to make such choices for me. I have discussed my desires concerning terminal care with them, and I trust their judgment on my behalf.

In addition, I have discussed with them the following specific instructions regarding my care:

(Please continue on back)

Date _____   Signed _____
Witnessed by _____   and by_____

The living will promises to be one major solution to the problem of passive euthanasia. But it is itself a source of controversy. Many people favor it because it enables people to determine their ultimate destinies and makes unnecessary a long court battle on their behalf when they are no longer able to speak for themselves. It is opposed by vitalists on the grounds that, in it, a person is possibly condemning himself or herself to euthanasia—in short, the person could be planning a future suicide.

During the time that the courts were considering the various cases, the states were also active. Beginning in 1976, thirty-eight states began to consider enacting passive euthanasia bills into law. Nicknamed "right-to-die" bills, they called for the withholding or the withdrawal of life-sustaining measures at the patient's demand.

In the years since they were first introduced, right-to-die bills have been passed into law in eleven of those thirty-eight states, among them California, Idaho, and Kansas. In the remaining states—and in a number of others that have more recently begun to consider similar legislation—the bills have run into stiff opposition from anti-euthanasia forces. The opposition has been so fierce that the bills have been either repeatedly defeated or put aside for future action in such states as Connecticut, Massachusetts, Ohio, and Virginia. In Connecticut, a right-to-die bill was narrowly defeated in 1979 and 1981.

The battle over passive euthanasia legislation is being waged by many of the same people who are active in the abortion controversy. This should not be surprising because essentially the same basic human rights are at stake in both these matters of life and death. The right-to-life forces in the abortion controversy are also much opposed to the right-to-die legislation; they include people of a conservative bent politically and a number of church groups and figures, among them many Catholics who, despite their church's stated position on passive euthanasia, still find it morally repugnant. The right-to-die legislation is supported by many abortion advocates because— just as they feel a woman should have the right to choose an abortion—they believe that a suffering and incurably ill patient should have the right to opt for death.

A SPECIAL PROBLEM

Though the living will promises to be a solution for many patients, it will be of no help in one special area of passive euthanasia. Namely, it will not help to solve the heart-breaking problem of what to do about infants suffering from and perhaps doomed to death by a grave birth defect.

Many people think of passive euthanasia as having to do only with adults, especially very old adults. Such is not the case at all. It can also concern newborn children.

The problem of newborn children with serious and possibly fatal birth defects is even more difficult to solve than that of adults. First, the infants can neither speak for themselves nor sign a living will. Further, many adults have lived long lives and are close to the end of their years when they fall incurably ill. It is easier to think of allowing elders to die than it is to think of permitting the death of babies who should have all of life in front of them.

Finally, when looking at some serious birth defects in their earliest stages, it can be difficult to judge just how much more serious an illness will become, difficult to judge if and when it will take the child's life, and difficult to judge just how much it will eventually interfere with the child's enjoyment of life.

These difficulties are causing both the medical and legal professions to consider a number of perplexing questions. Who should determine that a child is so defective that death is preferable to life? The doctor, alone or perhaps with the help of a medical committee and the parents? Or should the parents have the major or the only say? They are, after all, the ones responsible for the birth of the child. But can they be counted on to make the right decision? They will have to bear the burden of raising the child, and so there is the possibility of a selfish decision. Or should there be a special legal advocate for the child, one who speaks on his or her behalf when the decision to live or die is being made?

And *when* should the decision for life or death be made? How serious should a child's condition be for that decision to be made? How clear should the indications be that only death or a vegetable-like existence lies ahead? And how much medical treatment should be given a seriously impaired child whose chances of living are unclear but very likely poor?

On top of all else, there is the question of the right-to-die laws that have already been enacted. Giving a person the right to demand the withholding or the withdrawal of life-sustaining measures, they were written with an adult patient in mind. How can they be altered to provide for passive euthanasia in cases of doomed infants?

All these questions are not only being studied but are being heatedly debated in the medical and legal professions. As yet, there are no clear answers to them.

THE CONTROVERSY TODAY

And so the controversy rages today and promises to rage for years to come. In a handful of states, passive euthanasia has won legal status. In others, under their general laws against euthanasia, it remains a crime, if not in actual wording then by interpretation of those laws. And the states that are now considering right-to-life legislation have become battlegrounds for the pro- and anti-euthanasia forces.

Now that it has won legal status in a number of states, passive euthanasia seems to be gaining greater acceptance within the medical profession. In many areas of the country, its use is decided on a case-by-case basis, with the patient's condition, the patient's wishes, the family's wishes, and the doctor's opinion all being taken into consideration. But the situation is far from being resolved. Many physicians continue to oppose passive euthanasia on moral grounds and see it as a violation of their Hippocratic oath; but an increasing number of medical personnel feel that such matters as a patient's wishes and condition are more important. And the situation remains as yet unresolved at the hospital level. The policies of some hospitals make its use possible while the policies of other hospitals prohibit it.

No matter where it may be legal or illegal, passive euthanasia still poses a deeply troubling ethical problem for doctors who see it as a violation of their Hippocratic oath and their dedication to preserve life. Many in the medical profession are studying possible ethical and treatment criteria that one day may reconcile euthanasia with their Hippocratic oath and their dedication to life.

One aspect of this study is a search for a new and broader legal definition of when death occurs. At present, two definitions are used in the United States. Some states set legal death as the time when the brain irreversibly ceases to function. Other states see death as occurring when "all bodily functions" have ceased.

If you're a doctor who has already applied life-sustaining measures to a patient, these two definitions can place you in a legal-ethical quandary. In one state, on seeing that all brain activity has irreversibly ceased, you know that you're legally free to withdraw the extraordinary treatment, but you may be ethically reluctant to do so because there are still signs of life in certain other vital functions. But in another state, you're legally bound to wait for the very last vital function to cease before you can call a halt to the extraordinary care, even though you may feel ethically free to do so because you know that, beyond doubt, death is inevitable.

A single, broad definition of death would enable doctors to know more clearly when they could, legally and in keeping with their Hippocratic oath, withdraw extraordinary treatment. It might also, in some cases, enable them to withdraw it at an earlier date than is now possible.

In a 1981 issue, the *Journal of the American Medical Association* suggested that the problem might be solved by combining the two present definitions. The *Journal* suggested that death be legally defined as being *either* the irreversible cessation of the entire brain or the irreversible cessation of circulatory and respiratory functions.

A new definition of death would undoubtedly prove useful in those cases involving doomed patients who have willed their organs for transplant to others. There have been instances in which such patients have been made to linger so long that their organs were no longer of use. In one recent case, the parents of a doomed teenage boy (he was suffering a massive aneurysm in the brain with no possibility of recovery) wished to donate his kidneys in the hope of saving another's life. The doctors refused to withdraw the extraordinary care being given the boy. He died two days later of uremic poisoning, which rendered his kidneys unfit for transplant.

In time, a new legal definition for death may be established. In time, new ethical and treatment criteria for the withholding or withdrawal of life-sustaining measures may be developed within the medical profession. And, in time, legislation permitting passive euthanasia may be enacted throughout the nation. Together, these factors may solve the present controversy to the satisfaction of most people and see it, at least officially, ended.

However, another controversy may lie beyond—a controversy over active euthanasia. There are a number of thinkers today who argue that active euthanasia may well be a moral and humane act in cases of especially acute pain and suffering. It is doubtful that such thinking would be greeted with much public sympathy at present. As it has for many centuries, the world still views active euthanasia as a moral wrong, with people recognizing a great difference between the act of deliberately ending a life and the act of stepping back and allowing it to end in peace and dignity. But who can tell what the attitudes of future generations will be?

Passive euthanasia is making us face the question of whether or not we actually have the right to step back and allow a life to end. Active euthanasia will bring us to the far more terrible question of whether there are instances in which we have the right to take a life deliberately.

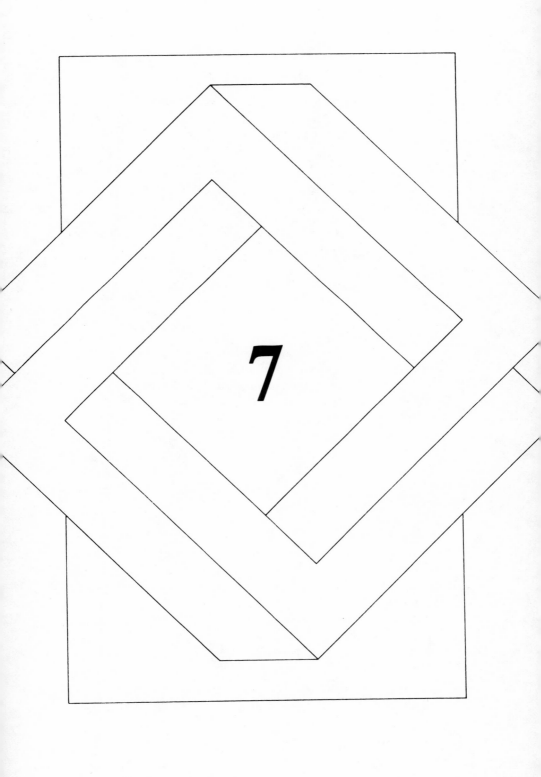

A NEW ROAD
TO BIRTH

Louise Brown was born in Great Britain in 1978. Three years later, in December, 1981, Elizabeth Jordan Carr was born in Norfolk, Virginia.

The two were very special infants, and they captured the attention of the world. The press called them "test tube" babies—children conceived outside their mothers' bodies. Louise was the first ever born in the world. Elizabeth was the first born in the United States.

But they are certain not to be the world's last "test tube" babies. Since Louise's birth, more than twenty such infants have been born in Great Britain and Australia. In late 1981, it was estimated that upward of 100 women throughout the world were pregnant as a result of fertilization that had taken place outside of their bodies.

The process that has made this new life possible, though it has been under study for years (more than ten years, for instance, in Great Britain), is still in its experimental stages. It is not used for all women who are unable to conceive through sexual intercourse but only in those cases where conception is impossible because a woman's fallopian tubes are blocked or otherwise damaged. Consequently, its usage applies only to a relatively few women. But it is bringing hope to all married couples with such a problem. And it is triggering a new controversy that is sure to grow as the procedure is perfected in the coming years and more "test tube" infants are successfully born of women with fallopian difficulties.

IN VITRO FERTILIZATION

Though widely used in the press and elsewhere, the term "test tube baby" is actually an incorrect one. To many people, it sounds as if the children are not only conceived but also developed in this item of laboratory equipment. Such is not at all the case. The fact is, test tubes have nothing to do with the process.

The correct term is *in vitro fertilization* (IVF), which means fertilization in a glass. The glass used is the laboratory petri dish. It is a shallow dish, usually less than an inch (2.5 cm) high, and is circular in shape. While in the petri glass, the female egg is fertilized with the male sperm.

Though IVF is a very precise medical procedure, it is easily described. In all women, the reproductive egg is developed in the ovaries. Doctors are able to remove an egg from the surface of an ovary by suction with special instruments. It is then transferred to the petri dish and placed in an incubator. In the dish is a nutrient medium that helps the egg to survive.

In natural conception, the female egg is fertilized in the fallopian tubes a short while after intercourse and then travels to the uterus, where it implants itself in the wall and begins to grow into a fetus. In in vitro fertilization, the egg remains in the incubator for several hours. Then the male sperm is mingled with it in the dish, with fertilization, it is hoped, to follow.

The egg is then watched for several days to see if cell

division of the ferti ized egg occurs. If so, the egg is returned to the woman's body. This transfer is accomplished by means of a tube inserted into the uterus via the vagina. The egg, protected by a shield of fluid and air, is placed in the uterus and implants itself in the wall. The normal stages of pregnancy then follow.

As mentioned earlier, the procedure is still in its experimental stages. In general, the chances of a successful fertilization and a successful implantation in the woman will soon be about one in five, according to the medical team at the Eastern Virginia Medical School at Norfolk, where the U.S. experiments are being conducted. It is felt that failures are principally caused by abnormalities in a fertilized egg—the very same cause of most spontaneous abortions in naturally conceived fetuses.

Should the first attempt fail to result in pregnancy, a woman may try it again. The doctors at the Eastern Virginia Medical School feel that the procedure has the greatest chance of success in women under thirty-five and have set that age as the limit for entering the program. In some cases, women up to the age of forty are accepted for the program.

THE BIRTH OF
ELIZABETH JORDAN CARR

In Great Britain, IVF had been under study and experimentation for ten years prior to the birth of Louise Brown. The work in the United States was begun at about the time that Louise was born. It is work headed by a husband-and-wife medical team—Drs. Howard and Georgeanna Jones.

Dr. Howard Jones is a gynecologist, and his wife is an endocrinologist. (Gynecology deals with diseases and disorders in women; endocrinology is the study and treatment of the endocrine glands.) Both physicians worked for thirty-five years in the field of human fertility at Johns Hopkins University at Baltimore, Maryland. In the 1970s, the couple retired to Norfolk, Virginia, only to be asked soon thereafter to head a group that would undertake in vitro fertilization studies and experiments at the Eastern Virginia Medical School. They accepted.

In the next months, childless couples came to them to participate in the work that would, it was hoped, lead to the first IVF pregnancies and births in this country. Among those couples were Roger and Judy Carr, he a mechanical engineer and she a teacher. In nine years of marriage, Mrs. Carr had suffered three losses in pregnancy, had undergone surgery as a result, and had been told that she and her husband had no further chance of conceiving a child.

Both Carrs, however, continued to want a child. Only one avenue lay open to them—the IVF program. They enrolled and, in April 1981, an egg was removed from Mrs. Carr, placed in a petri dish, fertilized with her husband's sperm, and returned to her womb two days later. The procedure proved a success. Elizabeth Jordan Carr, America's first "test tube baby," was born at Norfolk General Hospital at 7:46 in the morning of December 28, 1981.

A NEW CONTROVERSY

Elizabeth's birth was hailed as a medical triumph. But in the midst of this triumph and the Carr family's happiness, a strong note of dissent could be heard. Ever since the program was planned and launched, a number of people have objected to it. IVF has become the subject of a new controversy.

Because the procedure is so new and its success so recent, the controversy is not yet widespread. It is expected to grow, however, as future successes are recorded and an increasing number of IVF children are born. The attacks now being leveled against the procedure are, at their foundation, much the same as those being heard in the abortion and euthanasia debates.

Basically, three charges have been leveled against the IVF procedure. Let's look at them now, along with the answers that are coming in reply to those charges.

First, there is the belief that IVF is actually tampering with nature. The idea of conceiving a child in any but the natural manner strikes many as presumptuous and immoral, a violation of the way that nature or the Creator intended humankind to propogate itself.

This charge brings the reply that IVF does not attempt in any way to alter nature but simply seeks to assist it. The whole point of the procedure, as Dr. Howard Jones says of the program at Eastern Virginia Medical School, is to provide couples with a way of fertilizing the woman's egg when they are otherwise unable to do so.

It is further pointed out that no artificial substances are responsible for the fertilization. As in intercourse, the egg and the sperm are mingled. Only the locale in which they are joined—the petri dish rather than the fallopian tubes—is different. Then, once the fertilized egg is returned to the mother, pregnancy develops in the natural manner.

Elizabeth Carr's father, Roger, gave a more emotional answer to the charge that IVF is immoral. Speaking of the Jones program in a 1982 telecast in the Public Broadcasting System's "Nova" series, Mr. Carr challenged those who advocate this view to hold his infant daughter in their arms. How could they look down at her, he wondered, and think that anything immoral had been at work in the formation of this new and precious human life?

In the same telecast, Elizabeth's mother said that she had not even thought of the possibility of immorality being involved. As far as she was concerned, such thinking could be left to other people. All that counted was that she now had a daughter.

The second objection holds that the steps involved in the IVF process put the delicate egg at risk. The danger of damaging the egg and thus inducing abnormalities in the future child is great.

The reply here is that natural conception also involves the risk of abnormal fetuses. As was pointed out in chapter 1, the majority of spontaneous abortions are the result of abnormal fetuses breaking away from the mother. As in natural conception, there is the danger of abnormal fetuses emerging, but it is anything but a certainty. The birth of healthy children such as Elizabeth Carr and Great Britain's Louise Brown proves the point.

The third objection may well be the most substantial of all. It is the fear of genetic manipulation. As many people see it, there is nothing to stop doctors from tampering with the woman's egg. As the IVF procedure is perfected and more knowledge is gained about the art of forming life, scientists could conceivably begin trying to develop certain types or breeds of humans—perhaps "races" of servants meant only to serve their society, perhaps "races" of the super-strong and the super-intelligent who would be the masters of that society. The "brave new world" and the frightening population control that writers Aldous Huxley and George Orwell warned of many years ago could finally be upon us.

There can be little doubt that, if IVF fell into unwise hands, the dangerous practice of genetic manipulation might follow. But Dr. Howard Jones, speaking during the 1982 "Nova" telecast, replied to this fear with several comments.

He said, first, that the program at Eastern Virginia Medical School is dedicated to helping childless couples achieve pregnancy and that there is no thought of using IVF for other purposes. He then pointed out that certain safeguards have already been established in current IVF programs—advisory committees that look at all aspects of the programs and have the authority to disapprove any experimentation that promises to be dangerous or improper. It would be expected that future IVF programs would be similarly governed.

Finally, Dr. Jones mentioned what he sees to be the greatest safeguard of all. While admitting that human behavior can be difficult to regulate, he said that the principal deterrent to genetic manipulation is the integrity and the trustworthiness of the medical and scientific personnel involved in IVF work.

In addition to the objections being presently voiced, there is a legal problem that may have to be faced in the future. It rises out of the proposed constitutional amendment and the proposed Helms-Hyde bill that have taken shape in the abortion controversy. Both measures, as you know, seek to establish in law that humanness occurs at conception. If, in some future year, federal law does set humanness at this point, the legality of IVF and, in particular, one aspect of its work will come into serious question.

At present, IVF researchers are able to see when a fertilized egg begins to grow in an abnormal fashion. The reasons for the abnormal growth, however, are unknown to them. Studies are underway to find the answers to this and to a clearer understanding of the mysteries of human growth. These studies, currently being conducted with fertilized mouse eggs, could eventually lead to researchers using the cells of fertilized human eggs. Obviously, this work would see many of the eggs destroyed. If humanness at conception is eventually established in federal law, a fertilized egg will be declared a human being with all the attendant rights and protections under the Constitution, and the studies will be attacked as illegal.

Because no one can say when humanness actually occurs in pregnancy, any such federal law is bound to stir up further controversy in the area of abortion. IVF would surely be caught up in that controversy. Should this come to pass, what will happen to a procedure that has recorded such fine beginning successes and to its allied researches into the mysteries of human growth? It must be left for time to tell.

TWO OTHER AREAS

Now that in vitro fertilization is being widely discussed, two other "test tube" procedures may catch the public's eye and be added to the list of controversies. Though both are controversial subjects and though both have been publicly debated, they have thus far escaped widespread public argument. They are *artificial insemination* and *cloning*.

This is a medical procedure by which sperm is removed from the male and then injected by instruments into the female to cause pregnancy. The term *insemination*, which comes from the word *semen* (the fluid containing the sperm), means to implant that fluid in the female. Artificial insemination was initially planned for use in animals, but was then used in humans.

The first artificial insemination experiments, using several dogs, were conducted in the late eighteenth century by the Italian priest-biologist, Lazzaro Spallanzani. With these experiments, Spallanzani proved that certain microbes (the *spermatozoa*) in semen were responsible for fertilizing the female egg. Earlier, fatty substances that had been observed in semen had been thought to be responsible.

By the 1920s and 1930s, artificial insemination was being used successfully in the cattle and dairy industries of several countries, among them the United States and Russia. The process was considered a boon because the sperm of a superior bull could be used to impregnate several thousand females each year and thereby improve the quality of the herds and, consequently, the quality of meat and dairy products.

Cattle breeders and dairy farmers appreciated the process for yet another reason. They did not, as was required for natural breeding, need to go to the expense of keeping a large number of bulls.

Experiments early in this century established that artificial insemination could be applied to human beings. Couples who could not achieve pregnancy through intercourse could now bear children. Artificial insemination is often used at present when the husband is fertile (contains healthy, active sperm) but is impotent (unable to complete intercourse). Or the husband may be sterile (unable to fertilize because of a low sperm count or weak sperm). In these cases another male, called a donor, provides the sperm. The donor is usually unknown to the woman and is customarily chosen by the doctor. A man is sought who has a similar background to the married couple and who physically resembles the mother or the father, or both, so that the child will not be dissimilar to them in appearance. The potential donor is then closely examined to ascertain that he is free of genetic or other diseases.

Recent advances have also made it possible for artificial insemination to be used when a husband is fertile but his wife is incapable of becoming pregnant. Another woman is then chosen according to the same criteria that is used to select a male donor, and the sperm is introduced into her womb. The woman is known as a *surrogate mother* (*surrogate* means to take the place of another). The resultant child is raised by the husband and wife. Surrogate mothering is still rather rare.

It is not known exactly how many couples in the United States have produced children through artificial insemination, but the number is thought to be in the thousands. What *is* known is that the process has posed a legal question. It is the question of which man is legally responsible for the child when a donor, rather than the husband, provides the sperm. Recent court decisions and state statutes have tended to name the husband as the legal father. The question of who is the legal mother in cases involving surrogate mothers has yet to be decided.

Like in vitro fertilization, artificial insemination has been branded as immoral by a number of religious groups—and for the same reasons. It is seen by these groups as a violation of the way that nature or God intended humankind to propagate. The charge is also made that artificial insemination constitutes adultery when a male donor or a surrogate mother is used.

The people who favor artificial insemination view it in the same light as in vitro fertilization. They regard it as a great gift to the many men and women who want children but are unable, for various biological reasons, to conceive them in the natural manner. They feel, too, that in all cases—even in those involving male donors and surrogate mothers—the use of artificial insemination should be a matter of private choice.

As in in vitro fertilization, one aspect of artificial insemination is particularly upsetting for some people— the threat of genetic manipulation. The male sperm, on being removed, can be kept alive for long periods by freezing it. There is some fear that the sperm of men with outstanding genetic characteristics could be maintained in "sperm banks" and then, over an extended span of time, be used to fertilize many women and produce a breed or class of "super beings."

Scientists do not take this view seriously. They point out that fathers who have won great success and high public esteem often produce children who are not as talented or intelligent; the same is true of highly successful women. In great part, this is due to the fact that each parent provides only one-half of a child's genetic endowment and so some genetic weaknesses on either side may also appear in the child. Further, no child can be expected to be an exact carbon copy of either parent but will evidence individual traits of its own, some of them possibly weak. Finally, as does everyone, even the most successful human being carries genes that may well produce undesirable effects in a child, effects that can range from physical problems to learning disabilities.

And so scientists do not think that "sperm banks" would automatically produce a breed or class of "super beings."

CLONING

Cloning means the asexual (without intercourse) reproduction of a living thing that is identical in all respects to the parent. It is the primary mode of reproduction for bacteria and other unicellular (single cell) organisms. The offspring is called a clone, a name that comes from the Greek word *klon* and means *twig*.

Cloning is widely used in agriculture and horticulture to propagate varieties of plant life that might otherwise die out if left to reproduce themselves through seeds. This type of cloning is done by cutting and grafting. For more than two centuries, the process has kept such fruits as the Winesap apple and the Bartlett pear from disappearing.

Cloning is also used in the laboratory to produce strains of bacteria for study and scientific use. These strains are produced by using just one or a few genes from a plant, animal, or human organism. Scientists believe that these studies can result in such beneficial products as a bacteria that could be used in the manufacture of penicillin. It is felt that the studies could also lead to superior breeds of livestock, plants that are resistant to disease and drought, and bacteria that can be substituted for fertilizer.

Experiments in animal cloning have also been attempted. To date, most of the experiments have succeeded only when lower orders of animals, such as toads and rats, have been used.

The animal experiments—and the very idea of cloning, itself—indicate that it may be possible one day to clone human beings. This possibility has caused some people to fear that a breed of humans could be cloned to serve as slaves or soldiers for their masters. The idea has been spread by a number of recent science-fiction stories, motion pictures, and television dramas. A very popular example of such fiction was the book, The Boys from Brazil, which was also made into a film.

Today, there seems to be little substance to the fear. Higher orders of animals have proved resistant to cloning because their offspring inherit a wide-ranging combination of the mother's and father's traits. Yet it may be possible—by obtaining only certain genes or certain combinations of genes from the reproductive cells—to produce a high-order clone, even a human one. But this is for the future, the distant future. In general, science sees the cloning of humans as unrealistic for the present time.

But should human cloning become a reality as science advances in the next years, it will certainly become a subject of major debate. Cloning may well be one of the most critical debates in the history of humankind as it poses the question of whether we have the right to so alter nature that we can create a human being whose characteristics are of our own choosing.

Abortion, passive euthanasia, and in vitro fertilization—these, then, are the three great medical, moral, and legal controversies facing the people of the 1980s, with such other matters as artificial insemination and cloning perhaps to join them one day. We've looked at each in turn, have discussed the varying and conflicting positions that have been taken on each, and have attempted to explain the reasons why these positions are being taken.

They are all complex issues, and often cause such sharp conflicts between the senses of morality and compassion by which all civilized people try to live that they seem beyond a solution acceptable to everyone. And, indeed, they may well be beyond such a solution. But, as is true of any controversial issue, an attempt must be made to settle them in a manner that is at least satisfying to the majority of people.

Every citizen, as was said at the beginning of this book, can assist in that solution. This can be done, first, by deciding where you stand in each of the controversies, by then talking with friends about the issues and the positions being taken, by supporting appropriate organizations and individuals, and by informing local, state, and national representatives of your views.

It is hoped that this book has helped you gain a better understanding of these complex vital matters.

And they are indeed vital matters—matters of life and death.

RECOMMENDED READING LIST

If you're interested in looking further into the matters of life and death, you'll find the following books and magazine articles to be of particular help:

BOOKS

American Friends Service Committee. *Who Shall Live? Man's Control Over Birth and Death.* New York: Hill and Wang, 1970.

Barr, Samuel J., M.D., with Dan Abelow. *A Woman's Choice.* New York: Rawsom Associates, 1977.

Burtchaell, James Tunstead, C.S.C., editor. *Abortion Parley: Papers Delivered at the National Conference on Abortion Held at the University of Notre Dame in October, 1979.* New York: Andrews And McMeel, 1980.

Heifetz, Milton D., M.D., with Charles Mangel. *The Right to Die.* New York: G. P. Putnam's, 1975.

Jaffe, Frederick S.; Barbara L. Lindheim; and Philip R. Lee. *Abortion Politics: Private Morality and Public Policy.* New York: McGraw-Hill, 1981.

Manners, Marya. *Last Rights.* New York: William Morrow, 1974.

Nathanson, Bernard N., M.D., with Richard N. Ostling. *Aborting America.* New York: Doubleday, 1979.

Quinlan, Joseph and Julia. *Karen Ann: The Quinlans Tell Their Story.* New York: Doubleday, 1977.

Sloane, R. Bruce, M.D., and Diana F. Horvitz. *A General Guide to Abortion.* Chicago: Nelson-Hall, 1973.

MAGAZINE ARTICLES

"Abortion: The Battle of 'Life' vs. 'Choice.' " *Time*, April 6, 1981.

"The Attack on Abortion." *Newsweek*, April 6, 1981.

Coburn, Judith. "Abortion: Will We Lose Our Right to Choose?" *Mademoiselle*, July 1981.

"Here's What You Had to Say About Abortion." *Teen*, February 1982. Young people's opinions.

"The Last Word—Whose?" *The Christian Century*, September 6, 1981.

"Lifesaving Pioneer Christiaan Barnard Has a New Cause: Euthanasia." *People*, February 2, 1981.

"Morality, Law, and Politics: Abortion." *Commonweal*, November 20, 1981. Special issue on abortion.

Paris, John J., and Richard A. McCormick. "Living-Will Legislation, Reconsidered." *America*, September 5, 1981.

"Should Abortions Be Outlawed?" *U.S. News & World Report*, May 4, 1981.

Will, George F. "The Case of the Unborn Patient." *Newsweek*, June 22, 1981.

INDEX

[117]